To Katherine
With best wishes!
Hilary Giner-Sorolla.

A Christian's Treasury of Trees & Plants

Hilary Giner-Sorolla

Copyright © 2011 Hilary Giner-Sorolla

All rights reserved. No part of this book may be used or reproduced by any means, graphic, electronic, or mechanical, including photocopying, recording, taping or by any information storage retrieval system without the written permission of the publisher except in the case of brief quotations embodied in critical articles and reviews.

The views expressed in this work are solely those of the author and do not necessarily reflect the views of the publisher, and the publisher hereby disclaims any responsibility for them.

Verses of scripture are taken from the Holy Bible, King James version, printed by Oxford University Press, also the New Revised Standard Version, copyright 1989, Division of Christian Education of the National Council of Churches of Christ in the U.S.A.

All photographs and illustrations are by Hilary Giner-Sorolla, unless otherwise stated.

WestBow Press books may be ordered through booksellers or by contacting:

WestBow Press
A Division of Thomas Nelson
1663 Liberty Drive
Bloomington, IN 47403
www.westbowpress.com
1-(866) 928-1240

Because of the dynamic nature of the Internet, any Web addresses or links contained in this book may have changed since publication and may no longer be valid.

Any people depicted in stock imagery provided by Thinkstock are models, and such images are being used for illustrative purposes only.

Certain stock imagery © Thinkstock.

ISBN: 978-1-4497-0711-8 (sc)

Library of Congress Control Number: 2010938932

Printed in the United States of America

WestBow Press rev. date: 07/22/2011

INTRODUCTION

Whether you believe in them, or not, the legends surrounding trees and plants contain powerful images which appeal to us because of their humanity and sheer simplicity.

God employed a burning bush as a medium of revelation when He spoke to Moses, and every tree or plant on this planet is afire with His presence. For example, in the plant realm, the cornflower has ultraviolet pigments in its blue petals which are invisible to the human eye but irresistible to a pollinating bee. In the realm of trees, the seed of the maple is equipped with a neat pair of wings which enables it to sail away from the parent on a current of air. Jesus used trees and plants as metaphors, and early monks and missionaries took up the torch, re-labeling a number of trees and plants with holy names as an educational tool.

In this book, I have sought to rescue some of these legends from obscurity, concentrating on those within the Judeo-Christian tradition; in a few instances, I have taken the liberty of linking biblical references to botanical names. It is my hope that this collection, with its beautiful photographs and simple text, will reach a wide audience, to inform, inspire, and entertain.

DEDICATION

To my mother Esme Livingston Toy who surprised and delighted me when she requested a certain book for her birthday.

This work, heavily illustrated, which equated everyday life with the psalms, planted the seed of an idea which cumulated in the writing of this book, after many years, along with the classes of a gifted Botany teacher along the way.

ACKNOWLEDGEMENTS

Laurie Campbell, Scotland, U.K.	....	Nature photography, broom, common butterwort, common milkwort.
Daran Crush, England, U.K.	....	Nature photography, cowslip.
Paul Zimmerman, Ashdown Roses, South Carolina, U.S.A.	....	Permission to photograph moss rose.
McKinsey Printing Co. Tryon, North Carolina, U.S.A.		
Spartan Photo Center, Spartanburg, South Carolina, U.S.A.		
Sharon Johnston, Asheville, North Carolina	....	Nature photography, yellow flag iris.

HOLY PERSONAE

Aaron, high priest
Abraham, patriarch
Adam, progenitor of mankind
St. Agnes, martyr
Ahijah, prophet
St. Ambrose, bishop
St. Andrew, apostle, patron said of Scotland
St. Augustine of Hippo, theologian, bishop
St. Barbara, martyr
St. Benedict, theologian, abbot
Father Bernado, priest, hermit
St. Bernard of Clairvaux, theologian, abbot
St. Boniface, missionary, Primate of Germany
St. Bruno, theologian, abbot
John Calvin, theologian, reformer
St. Christopher, martyr, patron saint of travelers
St. Clothilde, queen evangelist
St. Dabeoc, priest, missionary
David, King, warrior, musician
St. David, archbishop, patron saint of Wales
St. Dunstan, archbishop
Eve, mother of mankind
Ezekiel, prophet
St. Finbarr, abbot-bishop
St. Fintan, abbot
St. Francis de Sales, bishop
St. George, warrior
St. Honaratus of Arles, abbot
Jacob, patriarch
Jesus Christ, Son of God, savior
St. John the Baptist, evangelist, martyr
St. John, apostle
Jonah, prophet
St. Joseph of Arimathea, disciple
St. Joseph, husband of the Virgin Mary
Joseph, pharaoh & hero of the faith
Joshua, prophet
St. Ladislas the First of Hungary, King & national hero
St. Lebuin, monk
St. Leonard, holy man
Martin Luther, monk, founder of Protestantism
St. Mark, apostle
St. Martin of Tours, bishop
Mary, virgin, mother of Jesus

St. Michael, archangel
St. Moalrubha, monk, missionary
Moses, prophet, law giver
St. Nectan, missionary
St. Nicholas of Myra, bishop
St. Patrick, missionary bishop & patron saint of Ireland
St. Paul, apostle
St. Peter, apostle
St. Philip, apostle
St. Regulus, monk, archbishop
St. Rita, nun
St. Stephen, deacon, martyr
St. Timothy, bishop
St. Veronica, disciple
St. Zenobio, bishop

God writes the Gospel not in the Bible alone, but also on trees, and in the flowers and clouds and stars.

Martin Luther, 1483-1546

Contents

ADAM'S NEEDLE (Yucca filamentosa) 1
ADDER'S TONGUE (Erythronium americanum) 2
ALMOND (Amygdalus communis) 3
ALOE (Aquilaria agallocha) 4
ANGEL'S TRUMPET (G. Datura) 5
APPLE (Malus pumila) 6
ARABIAN STAR OF BETHLEHEM (Ornithogalum arabicum) 7
BALSAM (Commiphora opobalsamun) 8
BEDSTRAW (G. Galium) 9
BLACKBERRY (Rubus fruiticosus) 10
BLEEDING HEART (G. Dicentra) 11
BROOM (G. Cytisus) 12
BURNING BUSH (Various) 13
CALVARY CLOVER (G. Medicago) 14
CANTERBURY BELLS (Campanula medium) 15
CARNATION (Dianthus caryophyllus) 16
CAROB (Ceratonia siliqua) 17
CEDAR (Cedrus libani) 18
CHRISTMAS FERN (Polystichum acrostichoides) 19
CHRISTMAS ROSE (Helleborus niger) 20
CHRYSANTHEMUM (G. Chrysanthemum) 21
COLUMBINE (G. Aquilegia) 22
COMMON BUTTERWORT (Pinguicula vulgaris) 23
COMMON RUSH (Juncus effuses) 24
COWSLIP (EUROPEAN) (Primula veris) 25
CROSS VINE (Bigonia capreolata) 26
CROWN IMPERIAL (Fritillaria imperialis) 27
DAFFODIL (Narcissus pseudo-narcissus) 28
DANDELION (Taraxacum officinale) 29
DATE PALM (Phoenix dactylifera) 30
DESIRE (Capparis spinosa) 31
DOGWOOD (G. Cornus) 32
DOUBLE DAFFODIL (G. Narcissus) 33
ELCAMPANE (Inula helenium) 34
ELM (G. Ulmus) 35
FIG (G. Ficus) 36
FIR (G. Abies) 37
FLAG IRIS (Iris pseudacorus) 38
FORGET-ME-NOT (G. Mysotis) 39
FOXGLOVE (Digitalis purpurea) 40
FRANKINCENSE (G. Boswellia) 41
GLASTONBURY THORN (Crataegus monogyna c.v. "Biflora".) 42
GRAPE VINE (G. Vitus) 43
HAZEL (G. Corylus) 44

HEN-AND-CHICKENS (G. Sempervivum) 45
HERB-BENNET (Geum urbanum) 46
HOLLY (G. Ilex) 47
HORSE NETTLE (Solanum carolinense) 48
HYSSOP (Origanus Syriacum) 49
IMPATIENS (G. impatiens) 50
IVY (G. Hedera) 51
JACOB'S LADDER (Polemonium coeruleum) 52
JADE (G. Crassula) 53
JERUSALEM SAGE (G. Phlomis) 54
JOB'S TEARS (Coix lacryma-jobi) 55
JOSEPH'S COAT (G. Alternanthera) 56
JOSHUA TREE (Yucca bravifolia) 57
JUDEAN SAGE (G. Labiatae) 58
LADY'S MANTLE (G. Alchemilla) 59
LAVENDER (G. Lavendula) 60
LEEK (Allium porrum) 61
LILY-OF-THE-VALLEY (Convalleria majalis) 62
LOTUS (Nelumbo nucifera) 63
LUNGWORT (G. Pulmonaria) 64
MALTESE CROSS (Lychnia chalcedonica) 65
MICHAELMAS DAISY (Aster tripolium) 66
MILK THISTLE (Silybum marianum) 67
MIMOSA (G. Mimosa) 68
MONKSHOOD (Aconitum napellus) 69
MOSES-IN-THE-CRADLE (Rhoeo spathacea) 70
MOSS ROSE (Rosa centifolia muscosa) 71
MUSTARD (Brassica nigra) 72
MYRRH (Commiphora myrrha) 73
OAK (G. Quercus) 74
OLEANDER (G. Nerium) 75
OLIVE (Olea europa) 76
PALMA CHRISTI (Ricinus communis) 77
PAPYRUS (Cyprus papyrus) 78
PASSION FLOWER (G. Passiflora) 79
PINE (G. Pinaceae) 80
POINSETTIA (Euphorbia pulcherrima) 81
POMEGRANATE (Punica granatum) 82
PRAYER PLANT (Maranta leuconeura kerchoveana) 83
QUAKING ASPEN (Populus tremula) 84
REDBUD (G. Cercis) 85
RED EVERLASTING (Helichrysum sanguineum) 86
RED POPPY (Papaver rhoeas) 87
RESURRECTION PLANT (Selaginella lepidophyllia) 88
ROGATION FLOWER (Polygala vulgaris) 89
ROSE (G. Rosa) 90
ROSEMARY (Rosmarinus officinalis) 91

"ROSE OF SHARON" ... Autumn crocus (Colchhicum autumnale) 92
ST. ANDREW'S CROSS (Ascyrum hypericoides) 93
ST. BARBARA'S HERB (G. Barbarea) 94
ST. BRUNO'S LILY (Anthericum liliastrum) 95
ST. DABEOC'S HEATH (Daboecia cantabrica) 96
ST. GEORGE'S MUSHROOM (Calocybe gambosa) 97
ST. JOHN'S WORT (Hypericum) 98
SAXIFRAGE (G. Saxifraga) 99
SCABIOUS (G. Scabiosa) 100
SEASONING HERBS...Mint (G Mentha); Anise (Pimpinella anisum); Cumin (Cuminum cyminum) 101
SELF-HEAL (Prunella vulgaris) 102
SNOWDROP (Galanthus nivalis) 103
SOLOMON'S SEAL (G. Polugonatum) 104
SPIKENARD (Nardostachys jatamansi) 105
STAR THISTLE (Centaurea calcitrapa) 106
STORAX (Styrax officinalis) 107
SYCAMORE (Acer pseudoplatanus) 108
TEREBINTH (Pistachia terebinthus) 109
THORNS & THISTLES (Various) 110
VERONICA (G. Veronica) 111
VERVAIN (G. Verbena) 112
VIOLET (G. Viola) 113
WALNUT (G. Juglans) 114
WANDERING JEW (Zebrina pendula) 115
WEEPING WILLOW (Salix babylonica) 116
WHEAT (G. Triticum) 117
WHITE LILY (Lilium candidum) 118
WOOD SORREL (G. Oxalis) 119
WORMWOOD (Artemesia absinthium) 120
YELLOW ARCHANGEL (Lamiastrum galeobdolon) 121
YELLOW GENTIAN (European) Gentiana lutea) 122
YEW (G. Taxus) 123

ADAM'S NEEDLE (*Yucca filamentosa*)

A New World plant, tall, with woody stem, sword-like leaves and a terminal cluster of creamy-colored flowers, it was given the name Adam's needle because of the spines on its leaves with allusion to Genesis 3:7:

> And the eyes of them both were opened,
> and they knew that they were naked; and
> they sewed fig leaves together, and made
> themselves aprons.

When God created Adam, he gave him all the potential necessary to fulfill His purpose. Adam, in his capacity as first man, was not aware of this potential until God gave him work i.e. naming the animals, cultivating a garden, and sewing together leaves to make a cover.

Simply waiting to discover the abilities hidden inside us will not cut it. We must actively apply the principle of work to become aware of our latent gifts.

ADDER'S TONGUE (Erythronium americanum)

A plant native to North America, with one species in Asia and Europe, adder's tongue is a low-lying perennial found in moist woodlands and mountains.

The name probably refers to the protruding stamens which resemble a snake's tongue. Other names given to this plant are dogtooth violet or trout lily, the latter because of the trout-like mottling on its leaves. The Bible mentions those who:

> "have sharpened their tongues like a serpent;
> adder's poison is under their lips."
>
> Psalm 140:3

Harsh criticism and carping are both hurtful and damaging. The Apostle Paul wrote:

> Let all bitterness and wrath, and anger, and clamor,
> And evil-speaking be put away from you, with all malice;
>
> And be ye kind, one to another, tenderhearted, forgiving
> one another, even as God for Christ's sake hath forgiven
> you.
>
> Ephesians 4:31-32

ALMOND (Amygdalus communis)

This tree was first grown in the Mediterranean area where its nuts were highly valued as a source of meal and oil.

Called in Hebrew "Shaked" (the awakening one), it is the first fruit-bearing tree to flower in the spring-time; those with white blossoms bear bitter fruit, and those with pink blossoms yield the sweeter kind.

The almond was once chosen to signal divine favor. Aaron's wooden staff bore blossoms and ripe almonds overnight, which announced that God had chosen him to be Israel's chief priest.

(Num. 17:8)

How often have we sought God's will for our lives? His answer may come to us as an inner conviction, or it may be outwardly conveyed in some dramatic fashion, like an unexpected encounter with an angel in disguise.

"Wherefore be ye not unwise, but understanding what the will of the Lord is."

Ephesians 5:17

ALOE (Aquilaria agallocha)

Aloe is a tree which grows in tropical Asia; not to be confused with the succulent in the picture. The tree is also known as eaglewood, agalloch or shoot of paradise.

In the East, according to legend, it is the only tree still in existence which grew in the Garden of Eden. Adam is said to have taken a shoot with him when he was banished.

Adam may have made a mistake when he ate from the tree of knowledge but his choice of the aloe for transplanting was a wise one. In Ancient Egypt the resin of the tree was used for embalming; In Ancient China, physicians used its medicinal properties to cure their rich patients. The use of the succulent plant, a descendent of the tree, by our ancestors as a burn healer, has carried through to the present.

ANGEL'S TRUMPET (G. Datura)

A plant originating in Asia having exceptionally fragrant pink, white, or yellow flowers which grow up to twenty inches in length. The word 'angel' comes from the Greek noun meaning messenger, but angel's duties extend even further than that to include praise, protection, comfort, judgment, and war against Satan.

Angels appear many times in the Bible. In popular imagination they are usually portrayed as gentle, placid spiritual beings, though this is misleading; they can move against evil with awesome power, even against nefarious nations.

> Make yourself familiar with the angels,
> and behold them frequently in spirit;
> for without being seen, they are present
> with you.

St. Francis de Sales.
1567-1622

APPLE (Malus pumila)

The apple tree grows in the temperate zones of the world. The first apples were small crab apples growing wild. Larger species have been found during digs around Neolithic lake dwellings.

Apples are mentioned in the Bible:

> As the apple tree is among the trees of the wood, so is
> my beloved among the sons. I sat down under his shadow
> with great delight, and his fruit was sweet to my taste.
>
> Song of Solomon 2:3

In later times, because people believed that Adam and Eve brought sin into the world by eating forbidden fruit in the Garden of Eden, it was common for writers and artists to depict this fruit as the apple; this is thought to have come about because the Latin word 'malus' means both apple and evil.

Some paintings of the nativity show the Christ Child extending his hand for an apple; this was meant to signify that He would be willing to shoulder the sins of the world.

ARABIAN STAR OF BETHLEHEM (*Ornithogalum arabicum*)

This perennial with creamy-white flowers is to be found in countries bordering the Mediterranean Sea. It was referred to in Biblical times as a lily and is, in fact, of the lily family, growing from bulbs.

There is a charming legend about how the Star of Bethlehem flower was given its name.

After the three wise men had entered the stable where Jesus lay, the star which had guided them exploded and fell to earth. Thousands of fragments hit the fields surrounding the town of Bethlehem and were transformed into these exquisite flowers.

Perhaps the shepherds, returning to their flocks after visiting the Christ child, doubled back, and told Joseph of this miracle, for it was said that he went out to gather some up, which he took to Mary.

BALSAM (Commiphora opobalsamun)

Balsam is a bush believed to have been grown from seeds mingled with the spices brought by the Queen of Sheba as gifts for King Solomon.

In ancient times, the bushes were grown on plantations between El Gedi and Jericho for use as a base for ointments and perfumes. When the Romans occupied Palestine, they sent twigs of balsam to Rome to symbolize their victory over the Hebrew nation. The conquerors prized this rare bush so highly, that an Imperial Guard was ordered to protect the plantations.

In today's Christian church, balsam is mixed with holy oil (chrism) and used for the anointing of altar stones, the sick; also at baptisms, confirmations, ordinations, and the occasional coronation of a king or queen.

BEDSTRAW (G. Galium)

Galium is a large genus of perennial herbs, with at least 400 species world-wide which vary in form and habitat. The flowers are either yellow or white.

Over the ages, the puffy stems of the bedstraw were used as bedding for cattle or to stuff mattresses. The leaves contain an enzyme which causes milk to curdle; this property was used as an aid by cheese-makers in earlier times.

According to legend, upon Christ's birth, the withered brown bracken lying about the Bethlehem stable became green again, and the flowers of the bedstraw, which had always been white, turned to a golden yellow.

The French painter Nicolas Poussin (1594-1665) depicted a nativity scene showing the bedstraw being gilded by the celestial rays streaming from the new-born Christ Child.

> For with thee is the well of life:
> and in thy light shall we see light.

Psalm 36:9

BLACKBERRY (Rubus fruiticosus)

The blackberry grows in both Europe and North America, mostly by the wayside where the soil is poor. It belongs to the rose family, bearing long, prickly canes.

In the British Isles, the blackberry is known as the bramble, and is linked to Michaelmas Day (September 29th) because on this date there was a battle between Satan and Michael the Archangel who sent his opponent tumbling down to earth where he landed in a blackberry bush. According to legend, Satan was so disgusted that he spat all over the bush, causing the fruit to take on a nasty sour taste.

To this day, it is customary not to eat blackberries after September 29th. It is also prudent, as they do indeed become unpalatable after that date.

BLEEDING HEART (G. Dicentra)

Bleeding heart is a perennial plant that originated in China and Japan. The puffy pink flowers have rounded spurs which make them look like a heart; below hangs a white tear.

Although the term "bleeding heart" has been used in an ironic sense for an excessive display of pity and concern for others, it brings to mind the term 'compassion'.

In the Bible, where is to be found the Parable of the Prodigal Son...described by Charles Dickens as "the greatest short story ever written", Jesus taught that compassion should be extended to include those who have offended us and become separated from us.

> And he arose, and came to his father. But when he was
> yet a great way off, his father saw him, and had compassion,
> and ran and fell on his neck and kissed him.
>
>   Luke 15:20

BROOM (G. Cytisus)

Thee are at least fifty species of broom. Native to Eurasia, this shrub has slender green stems with small leaves and yellow or white flowers. The seeds are in pods which dehisce with a loud pop when ripe.

According to legend, when Joseph and Mary were fleeing to Egypt with the baby Jesus, the Virgin cursed the broom because the dry, discarded pods made a crackling sound when stepped on, thus making the fugitives vulnerable to discovery by Herod's soldiers who were bent on slaughtering the Christ child who was born, according to the Wise Men, to be King of the Jews.

> In God have I put my trust; I will not be afraid what man can do unto me.
>
> Psalm 56:11

BURNING BUSH (Various)

There are four different North American species of burning bush. Classified as a shrub, it is a native of Eurasia.

The leaves are dark green through spring and summer and turn scarlet during the fall.

The answer to which of the actual species of burning bush through which God spoke to Moses in the Sinai, is controversial. The arid climate would not have supported the perennial that we in temperate climates know.

The monks of St. Katherine's Monastery on the Sinai Peninsula show visitors a bramble bush which they claim is a direct descendant of the burning bush Moses saw. However, experts think it must have been an acacia, the thorn of the desert, which is common in that part of the world.

The most interesting aspect of this miracle is that, though the bush burned with flame, it was not consumed (Exodus 3:1-14).

Perhaps, like Moses, there is a miracle waiting to change your life; have comfort in the knowledge that it will be ignited by the unquenchable spirit of God.

CALVARY CLOVER (G. Medicago)

This annual is native to the Mediterranean countries. It has carmine spots in the center of its green trifoliate leaves which stand for the Trinity. The spots themselves, stand for the blood which fell from Jesus' body onto clover growing beneath the cross.

Legend has it that Jesus' blood stained the soles of Pilate's sandals when he visited the site and was tracked away when he left.

The dried seed pods, when bent into a circle, are said to resemble the crown of thorns placed on Jesus' head by his captors.

Calvary, or Golgotha, is referred to in the New Testament as the hill outside Jerusalem where the crucifixion took place.

Jesus died in agony on that execution site, leaving behind a small band of bewildered disciples. However, it was because of His death and resurrected life that His power was unleashed and the barrier to God removed.

> And, behold, the veil of the temple
> was rent in twain from the top to
> the bottom; and the earth did quake,
> and the rocks rent:

Matt. 27:51

CANTERBURY BELLS (*Campanula medium*)

Native to Europe, this plant is popular because of its showy bell-shaped flowers which were so named because they resembled the small bells tied to the horses of Canterbury pilgrims.

Small bells were used before the dawn of Christianity. It was the custom to sew golden bells onto the hem of the High Priest's robe so that people could hear him as he moved about the temple. Bells make a statement every way you look at them. In the early life of the Church they were rung as a signal for assembly. Later, monks adopted the custom as a call for prayer. In the Twelfth Century, huge bells were cast and hung in belfries of the newly-built cathedrals to call an expanding population to worship services. During World War 2, the bells of Canterbury and all England were silent; they were only to be rung if there was a German invasion. Once the war was over, their joyful peal came to mean victory after a hard-fought struggle.

> Except the Lord keep the city:
> the watchman waketh but in vain.
>
> Psalm 127:2

CARNATION (Dianthus caryophyllus)

A perennial of the pink family, this plant is valued for its fragrant white, red or pink flowers.

There is a Christian legend that when the Virgin Mary was on her way to Calvary, this hitherto unknown flower sprang up in places where her tears hit the ground.

It was this simple story that inspired Anna M. Jarvis of Philadelphia to choose the carnation as the flower to be worn commemorating mothers and motherhood. Traditionally, one wears a white carnation if your mother has passed away, and a red one if she is alive.

It is worth mentioning that the whole idea for Mother's Day came about when this remarkable woman began to hold a memorial service annually after the death of her own mother in May, 1905. As well as suggesting to her own circle that they follow this custom, she wrote thousands of letters on this subject to people in high office. In 1913, her home state of Pennsylvania and the U.S. Congress voted to support the idea.

Mother's Day is observed in the U.S. on the 2nd Sunday in May.

> So let us not grow weary in doing what is right,
> for we will reap at harvest time, if we do not
> give up.
>
> GAL. 6:9
> NRSV, 1989

CAROB (Ceratonia siliqua)

Native to the Mediterranean area, this evergreen tree is best known for its long flat pods which contain hard seeds, also known as carob beans, barely enough to sustain the starving.

Scholars have identified the carob's sugary edible pods as being the husks on which the swine fed in Jesus' parable of the prodigal son.

(Luke 15:16)

It is also thought that the husks are the locusts eaten by John the Baptist in the desert region of Judea (Matt. 3:4). This has resulted in the carob fruit being named St. John's bread or locust pods.

> And call upon me in the day of trouble: I will
> deliver thee, and thou shalt glorify me.

Psalm 50:15

CEDAR (Cedrus libani)

This evergreen tree grows on the high mountain slopes of Lebanon, Turkey and Syria, sometimes to a height of 120 feet, with a girth of 40 feet.

Used in the construction of King Solomon's splendid temple, it has been prized throughout the ages because of its resistance to weather and insect larvae, and for being easy to work with.

Symbols of strength and beauty, the cedars are used as an example to demonstrate the power and majesty of the Lord, which exceeds even theirs.

> The voice of the Lord is powerful;
> the voice of the Lord is full of majesty.
> The voice of the Lord breaketh the cedars;
> yea, the Lord breaketh the cedars of Lebanon.
>
> Psalm 29:4-5

CHRISTMAS FERN (*Polystichum acrostichoides*)

The Christmas or dagger fern is native to the North American Continent; it's imprint has been found on ancient rocks and seams of coal, a mineral formed by fossilized plants many eons ago.

The early European settlers used to scour the December woods for this hardy evergreen to take home as a Christmas present or decoration. One can imagine them lifting it out of the ground after carefully digging around it with their hunting knives so as not to disturb the rootstock.

> Every generous act of giving,
> with every perfect gift, is
> from above...

>   Jas. 1:17
>   NRSV, 1989

CHRISTMAS ROSE (Helleborus niger)

This is one of the few plants which starts to bloom in early winter and continues to do so for weeks in spite of being glazed over with ice or dumped on by snow.

The waxy cup-shaped flowers are white, the evergreen leaves glossy. Other names for this plant are 'hellebore' and 'winter rose'.

In Medieval times, the Christmas rose was known as "The flower of Saint Agnes". This saint's feast day is January 21st. Martyred at a very young age, she was renowned for her purity, steadfastness and courage.

In France, there is a legend about a young bell-ringer called Nicaise. A native of Rouen, his soul was saved from damnation by the miraculous sight of these beautiful flowers blooming undamaged by a heavy fall of snow.

> For sin shall not have dominion over you:
> for ye are not under the law, but under grace.
>
> Romans 6:14

CHRYSANTHEMUM (G. Chrysanthemum)

Developed in China and Japan long before being brought to Europe, chrysanthemums are grown for their showy, ray-like flowers, and are also used for medicinal products or applied to insecticides. There is a Christian legend concerning the 'three kings of the east'; when they had reached the place where the star they were following stood still above their heads, they were confused; there was no commotion in the narrow streets of Bethlehem, it was just a sleepy little town. Suddenly Melchior signaled the caravan to halt.

"This is the right place after all," he announced. "Look over there. A shimmering white flower with a likeness to the star we have been guided by."

After the king had dismounted and plucked the flower which was a chrysanthemum, the stable door behind which the Christ child lay, swung open, the three kings entered. King Melchior placed the white flower in the babe's grasping hand. In the time that followed, it was obvious that this simple gift meant more to the Christ child than the lavish presents the kings had brought him.

> A man's heart deviseth his way:
> but the Lord directeth his steps.
>
> Proverbs 16:9

COLUMBINE (G. Aquilegia)

This showy perennial has red, white, blue or yellow spurred flowers; inverted, they look like a circle of doves. This similarity gave them the name columbine which is derived from the Latin word 'columbinus', meaning dove-like.

In St. Mark's gospel we are told that when Jesus came from Nazareth and was baptized by John in the river Jordan, a spirit descended from heaven in the form of a dove, and remained upon Him. This implies that the Holy Spirit is indeed dove-like and gentle but at the same time able to pass on wisdom and power.

> Do not cast me from your presence
> or take your Holy Spirit from me.
>
> Psalm 51:11

COMMON BUTTERWORT (Pinguicula vulgaris)

This plant, with its violet-blue spurred flowers, grows among the peat heather of Scotland. It catches insects which become trapped on a mucilage that covers the flat, fleshy leaves.

The butterwort has been connected through legend to the early British saints, especially to St. Moalrudha. The plant was believed to have sprung up wherever the tip of this holy man's staff touched the ground. This would suggest that he was a brave man whose travels to convert the pagans were widespread. Where or when St. Moalrudha received God's calling for this missionary work is not known.

Perhaps one of the best examples of a person who received God's calling is recorded in the New Testament.

> By faith Abraham, when he was called to go out
> into a place which he should after receive as an
> inheritance, obeyed; and he went out, not knowing
> wither he went.
>
> Hebrews 11:8

Reverting back to the early British saints, the Lord had to admonish St. Lebuin two or more times after his first calling before he agreed to forsake his own country to become a missionary to the Saxons.

Abraham's faith was strong, and he heeded God's voice right away, but for those like St. Lebuin whose faith was weak, it is not easy to obey God's call in order to fit into His divine plan.

COMMON RUSH (Juncus effuses)

In the plant world, a reed is any of various aquatic grasses with upright, hollowed stalks. Isaiah mentions both reeds and rushes when he describes how God will comfort his people (Isa. 35:7)

Rushes and reeds grew in profusion beside the Sea of Galilee and River Jordan during Biblical times. When bent by a strong wind, they were regarded as being a symbol of weakness.

In another passage, Isaiah, referring to Pharaoh, King of Egypt, described him as "a broken reed". (Isa. 36:6)

The prophet Ahijah predicted that "the Lord will strike Israel, as an reed is shaken in water". (1 Kings 14:15)

Jesus used the reed in a parable. He knew that the people had doubts about John the Baptist's faith because he had asked the question "...Art thou he that should come, or do we look for another?" (Matt. 11:2-3)

Jesus countered by saying to the multitude: "What went ye out into the wilderness to see? A reed shaken with the wind?" (Matt. 11:7)

Our Lord went on to defend the imprisoned John the Baptist who was full of self doubt, by naming him "my messenger"...greater than all the prophets.

COWSLIP (EUROPEAN) (*Primula veris*)

The cowslip was named St. Peter's Wort in the ancient herbals because of its resemblance to a bunch of keys, the badge of St. Peter, who, according to tradition is heaven's gatekeeper. Legend has it that a report reached this apostle that people were trying to get into heaven by the back gate; he was so upset when he heard of this sneaky behavior that he dropped his bunch of keys which turned into cowslips after they had plummeted down to earth.

Mankind has always questioned the existence of heaven. Christians know, however, that Jesus began his mortal life with a manifestation of glory from heaven in the form of messenger angels who appeared to shepherds minding their flocks in the fields around Bethlehem. Jesus left on Ascension Day in a burst of glory when he withdrew from this mortal realm and rose up into a heavenly one.

What are our chances of getting into heaven?

We have this assurance:

> Jesus said: Let not your heart be troubled;
> ye believe in God, believe also in me.
> In my father's house are many mansions;
> if it were not so I would have told you.
> I go to prepare a place for you.
>
> John 14:1-2

CROSS VINE (Bigonia capreolata)

This climbing plant grows to a height of 75 feet. Inside the thick stalk it hides the symbol of the cross.

There are about 400 different cross-shapes but their meaning is basically the same: the horizontal post stands for worldliness and death, the upright post stands for spirituality and the life force...both are inseparable.

The cross can also be expressed as a hand signal. Early Christians used their thumb to trace the sign of the cross on their foreheads as a statement of their own faith, and as a sign of recognition to each other. The early Christians also started the custom of tracing the sign of the cross with water on the foreheads of new church members as a baptismal rite.

CROWN IMPERIAL (Fritillaria imperialis)

Popular in Elizabethan and Stuart times, this bulbous plant has yellow, orange or red showy flowers.

Some of the corollas have spot markings, giving the flower its Latin name 'fritillis', meaning dice box.

According to legend, crown imperials, which retain water at all times, are symbolic of the residue of remorseful tears brought about for failing to bow down its head when Our Lord passed by. Throughout the New Testament, we are exhorted not to be unbending, but to take action and seize the day.

> Be careful then how you live,
> not as unwise people but as wise,
> making the most of the time,
> because the days are evil.

Eph. 5:15-16
NRSV, 1989

DAFFODIL (Narcissus pseudo-narcissus)

The origin of the English daffodil is found in the Mediterranean area. The Romans brought bulbs to England when they conquered that island nation primarily because the sap in the leaves was good for staunching wounds. Eventually, the bulbs were carried to North America by settlers.

We encounter daffodils and the season of Lent at the same time; this has given rise to one of their nicknames "Lilies of Lent". The bright yellow flowers are greeted thankfully as they signal the arrival of spring. Their connection with Lent, however, might well remind us that Lent, derived from the Old English word 'lengten' meaning spring, is not merely a time of fasting and giving up, it is far more a time for growing up.

> But grow in the grace and knowledge
> of our Lord and Savior Jesus Christ.

2 Peter 3:18
NRSV, 1989

DANDELION (*Taraxacum officinale*)

Native to Eurasia, this herb with its yellow-rayed flowers and deeply toothed leaves has spread as a weed throughout North America. The bitter leaves are edible and are sometimes used to spice up salads.

The dandelion is assumed to be one of the herbs the Israelites ate with the paschal lamb the night of the Passover prior to their exodus from Egypt.

These bitter herbs have become symbolic of trying times. Early Flemish and German artists incorporated dandelion leaves into their paintings as symbols of anguish.

> These things have I spoken unto you, that in me ye shall have tribulation: but be of good cheer; I have overcome the world.
>
> John 16:33

DATE PALM (Phoenix dactylifera)

During the 3rd Century, a legendary giant lived in Asia Minor who had a burning desire to serve the mightiest of masters. He worked for a king, and when that failed, he tried serving Satan; but that too was a great disappointment. After that, he sought Christ.

One day he was carrying a child across a ford aided by his staff which was made of palm wood. Half-way across, his burden became so heavy that his stout legs began to stagger and he had to struggle against the swift current to reach the far bank of the river.

When the giant complained about the weight he was carrying, the child answered: "Understand this, you are bearing the weight of the whole world on your shoulders. I am Jesus Christ, the master you have been looking for. I accept your service, and as proof of this, watch what happens when we reach the other side and you plant your staff on firm ground."

The giant followed the child's instructions, and when his staff miraculously became a tree with a plume of leaves and clusters of dates, he fell on his knees and worshipped Christ.

From then on, he was known by the name 'Christophorus' meaning 'Christ bearer'. He was later, martyred for his faith.

DESIRE (Capparis spinosa)

...the grasshopper shall be a burden, and desire shall fail...

Ecclesiastes 12:5

The original Hebrew reads that the caper bud shall fail.

Desire is a spiny, trailing shrub which grows in the Mediterranean region. The unopened flower buds, called capers, are pickled in vinegar and salt and used as a condiment to give savor to food.

Taste and appetite are among the first of the senses to leave the aging. In this youth obsessed culture, it is comforting to note that God promises those in the winter of life His continuing esteem.

> The glory of the young is their strength:
> the gray hair of experience is the splendor
> of the old.

Proverbs 20:29

DOGWOOD (G. Cornus)

There are fifteen species of American dogwoods ranging from medium-sized trees through shrubs to wildflowers.

Legend is connected to the tree. Up to the time of the crucifixion, the dogwood had been massive, the size of a full-grown oak. The wood of this tree was chosen to be hewn into the cross that Jesus was to die on because of its strength.

As Jesus hung on the cross, he sensed that the tree was very upset that it had been used for this cruel purpose, and promised that in future it would never grow high enough or straight enough to be used in this way ever again. Furthermore, its blossoms would be in the form of a cross, two long and two short petals, and in the center of the outer edge of each one there would be nail prints browned with rust and stained with red. In the center of the flower would be a likeness of a crown of thorns.

Other trees have been put forward as being the one to bear the distinction of providing timber for the cross, however, the dogwood holds its own as being the most popular legend.

DOUBLE DAFFODIL (G. Narcissus)

Double daffodil or jonquil are the common names for this hybrid with more than one layer of yellow petals.

According to legend, a crusader, after years of fighting in the Holy Land, returned home to Churchill village in the English county which is now called Avon. His wealth had been spent, but he did manage to bring his wife the gift of two rare bulbs of double daffodils which he had purchased on his way home. Sadly, he was never able to deliver the gift because his wife had been dead for four years. Visiting her grave covered with the blooms of the common primrose, the knight was so overcome by sadness that he tossed the rare bulbs he had brought his beloved over the churchyard wall. Throwing himself on the ground, he died instantly, stricken with grief. The double daffodil was said to flourish for centuries in a field adjacent to the Churchill graveyard.

> You who have made me see many
> > troubles and calamities
> will revive me again;
> from the depths of the earth
> you will bring me up again.

Psalm 71:20
NRSV, 1989

ELCAMPANE (Inula helenium)

A tall, coarse plant, elcampane is native to Eurasia, having rayed, yellow flowers, and bitter tasting roots and leaves.

In Medieval times it was used as the main herbal ingredient in a digestive wine called 'Potio Paulina' or 'Drink of Paul', an allusion to St. Paul's injunction to "Use a little wine for thy stomach's sake." However, its use was wider than that, the herb being called upon to to cure a variety of ailments, including sin.

Linking the herb to both recovery from illness and deliverance from sin brings to mind Jesus' encounter with the paralytic when the Judaic assumption that Yahweh alone can forgive sins was seen to be false.

> But that ye may know that the Son of man hath power on earth to forgive sins, (he saith to the sick of the palsy.)
>
> I say unto thee, Arise, and take up thy bed, and go thy way into thine house.
>
> And immediately he arose, took up the bed, and went forth before them all; insomuch that they were all amazed, and glorified God, saying We never saw it on this fashion.
>
> Mark 2:10-12

ELM (G. Ulmus)

A deciduous tree, valued for its shade, and linked to an Italian legend.

St. Zenobio of Florence was a bishop who led a very holy life and was venerated by his flock for raising a courier from St. Ambrose, and, also, a child, from the dead.

An astonishing miracle occurred after he, himself, had passed away. The year was 417 A.D. As the saint's corpse was being borne on a bier to the place of burial, it traversed the Piazza del Duomo where the press of the crowd was so great that it slammed against the trunk of a withered elm tree. Amazingly, the branches began to bring forth buds and leaves.

> For to one is given by the Spirit the word of wisdom;
> to another the word of knowledge by the same Spirit;
>
> To another faith by the same Spirit;
> to another the gift of healing.
>
> To another the working of miracles; to another prophecy;
> to another discerning of spirits; to another divers
> kinds of tongues; to another the interpretation of tongues.
>
> 1 Corinthians 12:8-10

FIG (G. Ficus)

The fig tree is native to the Mediterranean region; Spanish missionaries brought it to the New World.

In Palestine, the ripe figs were harvested twice a year, in spring around the time of the Passover, and in September, which was the time of the main harvest, when there was great rejoicing, and people celebrated with picnics out of doors.

Symbolic of the Jewish nation, Jesus used the fig tree in a parable, pointing out that a barren tree represented Israel's failure to produce the fruit of holiness. (Matthew 21:17-22)

FIR (G. Abies)

There are about 40 species of this spire-shaped evergreen tree throughout the world. Its spreading branches bear flat needles and erect cones.

The fir is mentioned in a legend concerning St. Boniface who lived in the 8th Century. Of English stock, he became a missionary, sailing across the sea to work in the Netherlands and Germany.

In folklore, there grew a massive oak at a place called Gaesmere, under whose branches pagan rites were preformed in honor of the god Odin. St. Boniface attacked this tree with an axe, and with the help of a mighty wind, was able to bring it to the ground where it shattered into four even pieces, much to the amazement of the crowd. Many of the heathen were won over to Christ after this miracle.

The following yuletide, St. Boniface led his followers into the forest; singling out a fir tree, he explained that it pointed straight upward to the Christ Child. He went on to tell the group to take fir trees into their homes every yuletide, as a token of their new-found Christianity. The fir lives, he said, when the skies are darkest, and has no stain of of sin like the pagan's oak. He asked them to celebrate God's love in the sanctity of their homes.

FLAG IRIS (Iris pseudacorus)

This plant which flourishes in marshes and swamps, has yellow flowers and sword-like leaves. It is linked by legend to Clovis 1, a Fifth Century king who was married to a Christian princess Clothilde. Clovis was a warrior who worshipped the heathen war god Woden. One day, he found himself trapped in a bend of the river Rhine along with his army, surrounded by fierce tribesmen who threatened to destroy them. At first, Clovis prayed to Woden for help; that didn't work, so in desperation he prayed to his wife's Christian deliverer. Soon after, he noticed some yellow flag irises growing in the middle of the river. Realizing that there were shallows at that spot, he and his warriors splashed across to safety. Circumventing the enemy, they rallied and went on to win a great victory.

On Christmas Day, the same year as the Rhine battle, Clovis was baptized in the cathedral at Rheims together with 3,000 of his followers. On his wife's suggestion, the three black toads on Clovis's battle standard were changed to three flag irises.

In later times, the stylized three-petaled iris, flor de lis in the Old French language, translated lily flower, was adopted by the King of France as his armorial emblem.

FORGET-ME-NOT (G. Mysotis)

This plant, known in Europe and Asia since earliest times, was eventually brought to North America where it escaped from cultivated gardens into the wild. It slowly spread as far north as Alaska where it was adopted as the state flower.

A story is told that when Adam went around the Garden of Eden naming all the plants on God's command, he carelessly missed this plant.

After he had made a roll-call to find out if the names he had given were acceptable, a soft voice close to the ground asked: "What about me?"

Dismayed that he had overlooked this delicate plant with its clusters of small blue flowers, he named it forget-me-not to ensure that it would not easily be passed over ever again.

> Brethren, if a man be overtaken in fault, ye
> which are spiritual, restore such a one in the
> spirit of meekness;
>
> Gal. 6:1

FOXGLOVE (Digitalis purpurea)

The graceful spires of the foxglove with its neatly placed tubular flowers is most often found in the informal setting of a cottage garden.

This plant is linked to a legend about Nectan, a lesser known Celtic saint associated with Brittany and Cornwall...but principally honored in North Devon.

The story goes that two men had stolen two of Nectan's milking cows. Catching up with the thieves, he attempted to convert them to Christianity, only to be silenced when they overpowered him and chopped off his head. However, this did not deter Nectan who picked up his head and walked away. The flower is said to have sprung up wherever Nectan's blood spattered on the ground.

> And they shall turn away their ears from
> the truth, and shall be turned into fables.
> But watch thou in all things, endure afflictions,
> do the work of an evangelist, and make full
> proof of thy ministry.
>
> 2 Timothy 4:4-5

FRANKINCENSE (G. Boswellia)

A gum resin is obtained from the frankincense tree by peeling back the bark and piercing the trunk to release a milky-white fluid which soon hardens into pale gold globules ready for harvesting. Frankincense resin gives off a sweet smell when heated and was used as one of four ingredients of the incense burned in the tabernacle.

(Exodus 30:34-38)

In ancient times, frankincense was very costly because it was imported a great distance from Sheba, the southern country of Arabia. It was regarded as one of the treasures of the Temple in Jerusalem which was the center of Israelite worship.

Chosen by one of the Magi as a gift for the baby Jesus, the spiraling smoke from heated frankincense was meant to signify the link between the human soul and heaven.

GLASTONBURY THORN (Crataegus monogyna c.v. "Biflora".)

Joseph of Arimathea was a rich, influential Jew who lived in the Palestinian province of Samaria. It was he who petitioned Pontius Pilate, at considerable risk, for permission to take Jesus' body down from the cross; afterwards, he arranged for its burial in a rock-hewn tomb he had reserved for his own corpse.

It is believed that Joseph of Arimathea was the Virgin Mary's uncle and that the boy Jesus may have traveled to Britain on one of his trading missions to obtain tin and lead.

Growing old and weary, it came to pass that Joseph rested, having arrived on one of his journeys at Glastonbury Tor in Somerset. Kneeling down to pray, he stabbed the tip of his staff into the ground. To his amazement, the staff immediately took root and budded, which he took as a sign from God that he must stay in this foreign land.

The staff grew into the progenitor of the Holy or Glastonbury Thorn, a type of hawthorn which blossoms twice...in early summer and around Christmas.

Joseph and his companions, using Glastonbury as their base, built a willow and mud plastered church, the first such structure on British soil, and preached the gospel, converting many to Christianity.

GRAPE VINE (G. Vitus)

In ancient times, over the main entrance to the Temple in Jerusalem, the Hebrews erected a gold-leafed image of a grape vine because they firmly believed that they were the chosen people, the vine of God.

> The vineyard of the Lord of hosts
> is the house of Israel...
>
> Isa. 5:7

Jesus showed His disappointment with the behavior of the House of Israel when he forced men from the same Temple. (John 2:13-17). In His eyes they were not the great nation that they claimed.

*   *   *

Jesus used the vine as a metaphor when He declared:

> I am the true vine, and my Father
> is the husbandman.
>
> (John 15:1-5)

In verse 5, when Jesus links believers with the vine's branches, He was declaring that they can only bear fruit if they depend on Him.

HAZEL (G. Corylus)

The hazel is a tree or bush common to Europe and North America. It bears edible nuts enclosed in a smooth, brown shell.

A story is told about Finbarr, an Irishman, educated by monks, who founded his own monastery near Cork, a town in the southern part of the Republic of Ireland.

Finbarr, now an abbot-bishop, was meeting with a fellow church worthy who asked him for a sign of God's presence. Finbarr knelt in prayer, and the hazel tree under which the pair were sitting, suddenly shed its springtime catkins which miraculously were replaced by nuts. Getting to his feet, the smiling Finbarr harvested some of this God sent bounty and gave it to his colleague.

> Before they call I will answer;
> while they are yet speaking, I will hear.

Isa. 65:24
NRSV, 1989

HEN-AND-CHICKENS (G. Sempervivum)

Also named houseleek, this succulent has a basal rosette of fleshy leaves, and sprouts pinkish or purplish star-shaped flowers. In the psalms there is a beautiful metaphor regarding God's shelter and protection.

> He shall cover you with his feathers,
> and under his wings shalt thou trust:
> his truth shall be thy shield and buckler.
>
> Thou shalt not be afraid for the terror
> by night; nor for the arrow that flieth
> by day;
>
> Nor for the pestilence that walketh in
> darkness; nor for the destruction that
> waiteth at noonday.
>
> Psalm 91:4-6

These words have a familiar ring; they seem to echo today's news. Jesus used the same metaphor when he expressed his sorrow at the terrible things that were going on in Jerusalem...

> "How often would I have gathered thy
> children together, even as a hen gathereth
> her chicks under her wings..."
>
> Matt. 23:37

HERB-BENNET (Geum urbanum)

This hairy Eurasian plant, also known as St. Benedict's Herb, has trifoliate leaves and five petals symbolizing the Holy Trinity as well as the five wounds of Christ. Depictions of the plant were often incorporated into architectural designs. In Medieval times, the herb was used as an antidote for poison.

According to legend, when St. Benedict was comparatively young, he was called to lead a community of monks, but his rules of conduct were so strict that some of the monks rebelled. One of the dissidents presented Benedict with a cup of poisoned wine, but when the saint blessed the cup it shattered into pieces and the wine was spilled onto the ground.

God shields from harm those for whom he has a divine plan.

> The Lord is my rock, and my
> fortress, and my deliverer.

Psalm 18:2

HOLLY (G. Ilex)

There are about 300 species of holly shrubs and trees worldwide. It is traditional for Americans and Europeans to decorate their homes and churches with holly at Christmas time. It is deemed ill-fated to bring holly into the house at any other season.

The ancient English carol "The Holly and the Ivy" perfectly describes The Christian symbolism of the holly.

> The holly and the ivy
> > When they are both full grown,
> Of all the trees in the wood,
> > The holly bears the crown.
>
> The holly bears a blossom,
> > As white as any flower;
> And Mary bore sweet Jesus Christ,
> > To be our sweet Savior.
>
> The holly bears a berry,
> > As red as any blood;
> And Mary bore sweet Jesus Christ,
> > For to do us sinners good.
>
> The holly bears a prickle,
> > As sharp as any thorn;
> And Mary bore sweet Jesus Christ,
> > On Christmas day in the morn.
>
> The holly bears a bark,
> > As bitter as any gall;
> And Mary bore sweet Jesus Christ,
> > For to redeem us all.

HORSE NETTLE (*Solanum carolinense*)

This toxic plant, native to the United States, with its wavy-toothed leaves and pale violet or bluish white flowers, is similar to the potato plant.

The earliest settlers named it 'Apple of Sodom' because it was one of the worst weeds that they had ever encountered. Not only did it have thorns on its stems and leaves but the root stocks grew deep into the soil and were very difficult to dig out. On top of that, grazing sheep liked to chew the round yellow or orange berries, thus spreading the seeds through their droppings.

Although the berries are the least toxic part of this plant, they should not be consumed by humans who might mistake them for small tomatoes.

Farmers found that it took more than one season to eradicate this pesky weed; it was hard work, like man trying to root out evil, hence they named it 'Apple of Sodom' after the wicked town in the Bible.

> For the upright shall dwell in the land,
> And the perfect shall remain in it.
>
> But the wicked shall be cut off from the
> earth, the transgressors shall be rooted
> out of it.

Proverbs 2:21-22

HYSSOP (Origanus Syriacum)

This woody plant grows about 26 inches high. It has small blue, white or pink flowers which bunch at the end of the stem. Hyssop is mentioned in the Bible in ten places. The twigs were used by Hebrew priests to sprinkle blood, water, or a combination of the two, during purification rites.

Hyssop was employed to sprinkle the people and the book of the law during the sealing of the covenant at Sinai. (Hebrews 9:19) It was also utilized to pass a vinegar-soaked sponge to Jesus' lips when He was hanging on the cross. (John 19:29)

In Psalm 51:7, King David used the plant metaphorically when asking God to purify his heart after committing adultery and murder.

> Purge me with hyssop, and I
> shall be clean: wash me and
> I shall be whiter than snow.

Only God the Father and God the Son, can cleanse the guilty.

IMPATIENS (G. impatiens)

This showy annual is popular for use in planters, window boxes, hanging baskets and beds. The red, pink or white flowers bloom all summer long.

The plant gets its name from the Latin 'impatiens', meaning impatient, because the pods burst open and release the seeds as soon as they are ripe.

The Bible warns against impatience in several places. This negative trait does not belong to God who understands our human weaknesses and gives us a second chance over and over again.

> Better is the end of a thing than its
> > beginning;
> the patient in spirit are better than the
> > the proud in spirit.
>
> Do not be quick to anger,
> > for anger lodges in the bosom of
> > > fools.

> > > > > > Eccl. 7:8-9
> > > > > > > NRSV, 1989

IVY (G. Hedera)

There are fifteen species of the evergreen ivy, a ground creeper and climbing plant.

Apart from being a symbol of everlasting life, the ivy also was thought to symbolize faithfulness and friendship because of the ability of the rootlets along its stem to cling to rough surfaces.

> A man that hath friends must shew himself
> friendly: and there is a friend that sticketh
> closer than a brother.
>
> Provergs 18:24

After the death of Jesus, the word "brother" became the term used for a fellow Christian regardless of parentage, race or social status.

> A new commandment I give unto you,
> That ye love one another; as I have loved
> you, that ye also love one another.
>
> John 13:34

JACOB'S LADDER (*Polemonium coeruleum*)

This hardy perennial with pale blue flowers and numerous paired leaflets grows in wild, waste places to a height of 1-3 feet. It is named after an incident in the Book of Genesis when Jacob the Patriarch saw a ladder reaching up to heaven with angels descending and ascending while the voice of God promised him the land on which he lay, both to him, and his descendants...all while he slept, during a dream.

References to dreams are common in both the Old and New Testaments, and it is interesting to note that one of the jobs of the Hebrew priests was to interpret dreams. Jacob, however, did not need an interpreter for his dream: during a time of anxiety, God had reassured him that He was never far away.

> And he said, Hear now my words:
> If there be a prophet among you,
> I the Lord will make myself known
> unto him in a vision, and will speak
> unto him in a dream.
>
> Numbers 12:6

JADE (G. Crassula)

Jade is a small, succulent house plant from South Africa. It has a thick trunk and spreading branches.

The Chinese, honoring a Feng Shui tradition, put this plant on their windowsills to attract good fortune. This practice gave it a second name, money plant. In the West, it is supposed to bring a financial windfall if received as a gift.

Simply waiting for money to fall into your lap is the opposite of what Jesus spoke of in the parable of the talents and rewards. (Matt. 25:14-30).

In New Testament times, one talent was a unit of money (not actually minted), equivalent to 6,000 drachmas. In Jesus' parable, talents also stand for mental aptitude, so that a person with but one talent is not exactly short-changed and should be able to use good stewardship in order to reap a reward.

JERUSALEM SAGE (G. Phlomis)

This hardy plant, which can be found in the mountains of Syria and Turkey, has large heart-shaped leaves and creamy-yellow flowers which occur in whorls around the tall stem.

Being tolerant of harsh conditions, the plant is appropriately named after Jerusalem, the ancient and modern-day capital of Israel which has survived for centuries in spite of destruction and conquest. Jesus wept over Jerusalem, and later rode in triumph through its streets. On the Day of Pentecost, the Church was founded within its walls. The first martyrdom took place there when Stephen was condemned by the city council and dragged outside to be stoned.

> Pray for the peace of Jerusalem:
> they shall prosper that love thee.
>
> Peace be within thy walls, and
> prosperity within thy palaces.
>
> Psalm 122:6-7

JOB'S TEARS (*Coix lacryma-jobi*)

Originating in tropical Asia, Job's tears is a grass which can be harvested as a nutritious cereal, or used to make decorative beads. The tear-drop shape of the hard, white grains gave rise to the name Christ's or Job's tears.

The Bible is awash with tears; and suffering has never been expressed more vividly as in the Book of Job.

> My face is foul with weeping, and on my
> eyelids is the shadow of death.

Job 16:16

Job learned to live with the world as it is, and to worship God as He is, before there was a happy ending to his suffering.

There is a touching scene in the New Testament where Jesus wept as He stood by his friend Lazarus' grave, even though he knew that He possessed the power to raise him from the dead. This revelation of Christ's sympathy for those who have lost a loved one is backed up by His own words:

> Blessed are those that mourn:
> for they shall be comforted.

Matt. 5:4

JOSEPH'S COAT (G. Alternanthera)

This bushy plant from South America belongs to the amaranthaceae family. It's multi-colored leaves range from dark red to green. It's non-scientific name was inspired by the Bible story of Joseph's colorful coat.

Joseph, son of Jacob, one of the twelve sons of Israel, was a boastful and insensitive youth in the eyes of his brethren. He was Jacob's favorite and became hated even more when his father presented him with a coat of many colors. This so infuriated his brothers that they faked his death and sold him into slavery.

Joseph prospered in the land of Egypt, and the story comes full circle with his loving act of pardon.

> And he fell upon his brother Benjamin's
> neck, and wept; and Benjamin wept
> upon his neck.
>
> Moreover he kissed all his brethren,
> and wept upon them: and after that
> his brethren talked with him.
>
> Gen. 45:14-15

JOSHUA TREE (Yucca bravifolia)

This is a tree-like plant of the lily family which is native to the West and South West of the United States. It grows from 10-30 feet high.

Mormon pioneers named the plant-tree after Joshua, who succeeded Moses as leader of the Exodus, because its extended branches reminded them of an arm pointing the way to the Promised Land.

> And the Lord said unto Joshua,
> stretch out the spear that is in
> thy hand toward Ai; for I will give
> it into thy hand. And Joshua stretched
> out the spear that he had in his hand
> toward the city.

Joshua 8:18

In the same way, God does not leave us to fight our battles alone; if we put our trust in Him, He will show us a strategy that will lead to victory.

JUDEAN SAGE (G. Labiatae)

According to ancient tradition, the angled stems of the Judean sage inspired the design for the seven-branched menorah which was taken to the Temple in Jerusalem.

Biblical scholars believe it is this plant which is alluded to in the Book of Exodus.

> He also made the lampstand of pure gold.
> The base and the shaft of the lampstand
> were made of hammered work; its cups,
> its calyxes, and its petals were of one piece
> with it.
>
> There were six branches going out of its
> sides, three branches of the lampstand
> out of the other side of it.

NRSV Ex. 37:17-18

Art, music, poetry, literature, all feed on nature for inspiration, nature that is divine.

John Calvin, the French theologian and religious reformer who lived From 1509 – 1564, declared:

> "There is not one color, not one blade of grass,
> that was not created to make man rejoice."

LADY'S MANTLE (G. Alchemilla)

The botanical name for this plant is worth noting, being a version of the Arabic that alludes to the fact that its juices were used in alchemy, a pseudo-science practiced by the Ancient Egyptians. In the year 485, during the time of the Byzantine Empire, the so-called "Mantle of the Mother of God "was brought to a church in Constantinople where it was preserved as a holy relic in a transparent jar. Pilgrims flocked from far and wide to this shrine, many claiming that they received miraculous cures at the end of their journey.

Was this the reason alchemilla became Lady's Mantle in Christian eyes? Or was it simply that the dark green leaves with their crinkled edges and deep folds reminded people of a mantle?

The healing relic was lost when the Crusaders pillaged Constantinople in 1204, and alchemy as an elixir to ward off diseases lost favor during the Medieval period. But the immortal words of Jesus "...if thou canst believe, all things are possible to him that believeth." (Mark 9:23) are as powerful today as they ever were as a tool for healing.

LAVENDER (G. Lavendula)

Lavender is an aromatic herb with a Christian legend attached. It is said that the Virgin Mary washed the clothes of the baby Jesus and laid them out to dry on some low-lying bushes. When she returned to retrieve the clothes, she found that they possessed a sweet, refreshing fragrance from the spikes of purple flowers. One can imagine Mary's surprise and joy when she made this discovery. And so it is in our lives; happiness is found more often when it is not being actively pursued.

> But let the righteous be glad; let them
> rejoice before God:
> yea, let them exceedingly rejoice.

Psalm 68:3

LEEK (Allium porrum)

On the first day of March it became the custom for the Welsh to wear leeks to honor their patron saint, David. This 6th Century monk was born of noble stock. He became an archbishop and founded a number of monasteries.

The tale is told that when Saxon invaders threatened David's Welsh territory, he prayed for victory against them. Prior to the battle, he told the soldiers to dig up wild leeks to wear on their caps so that they could identify one another. The Welsh were victorious and continued the custom in David's memory.

In 1911, at the investiture of Edward, Prince of Wales, the leek was replaced by the more socially acceptable daffodil as the national plant symbol of Wales.

> By you I can crush a troop,
> And by my God I can leap over a wall.
>
> 2 Sam. 22:30
> NRSV, 1989

LILY-OF-THE-VALLEY (Convalleria majalis)

This plant, with its delicate white bell-shaped flowers, likes moist soil and a shady environment.

One of the best known legends of the Middle Ages was about the valiant warrior St. George who single-handedly slew a dragon with his magic sword.

A lesser known dragon story comes from Sussex, England and is linked to the lily-of-the-valley. Leonard, a holy man, engaged the fierce dragon Sin in combat. They fought face to face through a wood for three days. Struck, time and time again by the beast's sharp claws, spots of Leonard's blood dotted the woodland floor. Impressed by the unyielding fight put up by the saint, heaven blessed the spots of his blood.

In time, lilies-of-the-valley grew out of these sanctified specks, enabling pilgrims to trace the tide of battle.

> Wherefore take unto you the whole
> armour of God, that you may be able
> to withstand in the evil day, and having
> done all, to stand.

Ephesians 6:13

LOTUS (Nelumbo nucifera)

The lotus has its roots anchored in mud, and its stem partially submerged in brackish water, yet the flower grows above all this to a height of six to eight feet with flawless beauty.

Christians in the Far East have adopted the lotus as a symbol that we should try to live our lives untouched by corruption.

> For where envying and strife is,
> there is confusion and every evil
> work.
>
> James 3:16

LUNGWORT (G. Pulmonaria)

Also called Bethlehem sage because it is linked in folklore to the Virgin Mary.

The spots on the long-stalked leaves are said to be the stains from her tears at the crucifixion. Her eyes were believed to be as blue as the open flower; the pink buds were thought to represent her eyelids, swollen from weeping.

> ...weeping may endure for a night,
> but joy cometh in the morning.
>
> Psalm 30:5

MALTESE CROSS (Lychnia chalcedonica)

This perennial got its name because of its scarlet cross-shaped flowers, and the fact that a true-red cross is the symbol of the Mediterranean island of Malta with its history of chivalry and bravery.

In 1530, Emperor Charles V of France bequeathed the island to the Knights Hospitalers of St. John. Adopting the title of Knights of Malta, they defended themselves against Turkish attack in the famous Siege of Malta in 1565. Their rule lasted to 1798. During World War 2, while the Axis armies were assaulting North Africa, planes from Malta harassed supply ships bound for Tripoli. In retaliation, the island was under constant bombardment from Axis planes. As bombs dropped, the population of the island huddled in caves, and the British planes were safely sheltered in underground hangars.

The island managed to hold out, however, with the help of supplies and ammunition brought over from England by submarine. Malta's citizens were awarded the George Cross medal for gallantry.

> In famine he shall redeem thee from death;
> and in war from the power of the sword.
>
> Job 5:20

MICHAELMAS DAISY (Aster tripolium)

This plant is a wild species of the Aster family with its daisy-like purplish flowers which bloom from late summer through fall. They are at their best around September 29, the date chosen by the church to celebrate the Festival of St. Michael the Archangel, leader of the celestial host.

In Jude 9 the Bible alludes to a Jewish tradition concerning a fight St. Michael had with the devil over Moses' body because of his responsibility for burying the dead. As they argued, even Michael did not dare to declare the devil guilty, he left that to God.

During times of struggle and stress it is better to leave the outcome in God's capable hands.

MILK THISTLE (*Silybum marianum*)

The milk thistle, with its white-veined leaves, has been linked through folklore with the mother's milk of the Virgin Mary. It follows that other names for this plant are Our Lady's thistle and Blessed thistle.

Before it is born, and afterwards, through breast feeding, a baby borrows from its mother, the marrow of her bones, the calcium of her teeth…and, thereafter, it borrows from life.

In the Old Testament, a son was born to Hannah after many years of prayer. Naming him Samuel, she gave him up into God's service as a form of gratitude.

All possessions, offspring, health, sustenance, beauty, knowledge, love, friendship, talents, time and opportunity are lent by God, and we are entrusted to repay each one of them nobly and generously.

> For this child I prayed; and the
> Lord hath given me my petition
> Which I asked of Him:
> Therefore also I have lent him to
> the Lord.
>
> 1 Samuel 27, 28

MIMOSA (G. Mimosa)

Mimosa is a genus of leguminous trees, shrubs and plants which grow in warm climates. They have ball-shaped heads of pink or white flowers.

The legend goes that around 400 A.D. St. Honoratus founded a monastery on an island off the French Riviera. Margaret, his sister, converted from paganism in answer to her brother's prayers, came to settle on a nearby island so as to be near him. She made him promise that he would visit her once a year when the mimosa was in bloom.

Unfortunately, when the time came that she urgently needed his guidance, the flowering of the mimosa was two months away. As she prayed for God's help, her nostrils were assailed by a heady perfume. Looking around her she spotted a mimosa tree in full bloom. Getting up from her knees, she yanked off a branch which she sent to her brother. He promptly obeyed her call.

> Now that you have purified your souls
> by your obedience to the truth so that
> you have genuine mutual love, love one
> another deeply from the heart.

1 Peter 1:22
NRSV, 1989

MONKSHOOD (Aconitum napellus)

This perennial plant is native to Northern Europe and has purple-lilac, hooded flowers.

In pagan times, this plant was named wolfsbane because hunters killed the carnivorous beasts with arrows poison-tipped with its juices. Associated with witches because of its poisonous properties, the Church renamed it 'monkshood' at St. Dunstan's canonization to commemorate a prophetic dream the Saxon said had wherein he saw many monk's cowls hanging on a massive tree; this had encouraged him to put into action the founding of new monasteries and the re-founding of former monasteries razed to the ground by the invading Danes.

> And Micaiah said, As the Lord liveth, what the Lord said unto me, that will I speak.
>
> 1 Kings 22:14

MOSES-IN-THE-CRADLE (*Rhoeo spathacea*)

This house plant comes from Central America; it has rosettes of stiff, waxy leaves, and tiny white flowers which nestle in the axils, hidden in cradle-like bracts.

While a baby, the Hebrew Moses was placed on the waters of the River Nile in a floating ark only to be rescued by a member of the Egyptian royal family in whose household he spent his formative years. His given name, Moses, meant in Hebrew "drawn out" which would indicate that his destiny to be a great leader who would draw out his own Hebrew people from bondage in Egypt was set in motion from the beginning according to God's plan.

> For I know the thoughts that I think towards you, saith the Lord, thoughts of peace, and not evil, to give you an expected end.
>
> Jeremiah 29:11

MOSS ROSE (*Rosa centifolia muscosa*)

The moss rose goes back in time, being one of the four known species in the 16th Century.

According to German legend, a weary angel fell asleep in the shade of this plant with its fragrant pink flowers. When he finally opened his eyes, he thanked the rose for its hospitality and asked if there was anything he could do in return. When the rose was unable to come up with an answer, the angel then performed a miracle, causing a mossy veil to cover the flower stalk and the calyx. This characteristic acts as a protection, and has given the moss rose its name.

> For he shall give his angels charge over thee, to keep thee in all thy ways.
>
> Psalm 91:11

MUSTARD (Brassica nigra)

The black mustard is the most common of the many varieties found in the Middle East. It is a herb related to the cabbage. The seeds, which can be crushed to make a condiment, grow in slender pods. The seed, which is minute, grows rapidly into a mature plant.

When Jesus taught the disciples the Parable of the Mustard Seed, it was a lesson about faith. (Matthew 17:19-20)

They had just failed to cure a boy who was possessed by a demon and they asked Jesus the reason why.

Jesus replied that it was because their faith was weak and that if they improved the quality of their faith, even if it was as small as a mustard seed, nothing would be impossible to achieve.

Within every human being lies the potential do to powerful things and to grow rapidly like the mustard see, energized by faith.

MYRRH (Commiphora myrrha)

Myrrh is a fragrant gum resin extracted by small incisions in the bark of a small, thorny tree that grows in Yemen, Somalia and Ethiopia.

In ancient times, myrrh was a luxury item used in the preparation of the ointment with which kings were anointed. When one of the Magi chose myrrh as a gift for the baby Jesus, it indicated his future kingship. Used to preserve a corpse, this gift of the Magi visitor is also thought to have foretold the costly manner in which Jesus' body was prepared for burial. (John 19:39)

During the 4th century, myrrh was featured in a legend about St. Nicholas, bishop of Myra, a place on the coast of Turkey, present-day name Kale. Although the saint is identified with the legend of Santa Claus, there is a lesser known legend that people are healed by myrrh in its liquid form which miraculously spills out from his sacred relics and icons, even in modern times.

OAK (G. Quercus)

There is a story passed down from Renaissance Italy about a devout hermit, Father Bernado, who sat praying and meditating all day outside his hut under a mighty oak tree which he often talked to and fed with water. A compassionate vine-dresser who lived close by would send his child Mary to the hermit with gifts of food. The grateful recipient called the oak and Mary his two daughters...one that was dumb, and one that spoke.

There came a time when there was a great flood which swept away Father Bernado's hut so that he had to seek safety in the branches of the oak tree. When Mary found him, he had been up there for three days, numb with cold, and starving. She rescued him and took him to her home where he sheltered until his hut could be rebuilt. The old man prayed that Mary and the sturdy oak, who had both played a part in his deliverance from death, might be blessed in some special way.

In due course, Father Bernado died, and Mary, now an attractive woman, married. Furthermore, Mary's father cut down the oak and converted the wood into casks.

A young artist, Raphael, had been searching for the perfect model for a Madonna. One day, he knew his quest was over when he spied Mary, now a mother, seated on a low chair holding her baby boy on her lap. Just then, Mary's elder son ran to her side with a little cross made of sticks. Inspired by the moment, Raphael grabbed the lid of one of Mary's father's casks which were standing nearby, took out chalk and made a sketch of the scene on its smooth surface, which he later converted into a world famous oil painting: "Madonna of the Chair."

Thus the prayers of Father Bernado were answered because the Oak tree and Mary had brought beauty into the world.

> The Lord is far from the wicked:
> but he heareth the prayer of the
> righteous.
>
> Proverbs 15:29

OLEANDER (G. Nerium)

The oleander is an evergreen shrub with oblong, leathery leaves, and white, rose, or purple flowers.

In Spanish folklore, there is a story about a peasant woman whose daughter was critically ill. Nothing worked to restore the young patient to health, so as a last resort, the mother knelt down to pray, invoking God's faithful servant St. Joseph, patron saint of homes and families.

Suddenly, the room was flooded with rose light, and a man's figure was seen bent over the girl placing a flowering branch of oleander on her breast. Immediately after this was done, both the man and the rosy light faded away.

Soon, the girl began to recover and was eventually restored to full health. Word of this miracle spread, and the oleander was adopted as St. Joseph's flower.

> And call upon me in the day of trouble:
> I will deliver thee, and thou shalt glorify
> me.
>
> Psalm 50:15

OLIVE (Olea europa)

In ancient times, the olive tree was prized for its oil. The fruits were harvested late, in October and November, and their oil extracted to be used in cooking and lighting.

The parable of the Golden Candlestick (menorah) in the Book of Zechariah (4:1-14) depicts two olive trees. An inexhaustible supply of golden oil flows from their fruits through feeding pipes to a seven-branched golden candlestick from which emanates light. This parable reminds us that the Holy Spirit, represented by the olive oil, is channeled to us directly from God. With it, we can become what He wants us to be, an exceptional person, a bright light.

> (Until) the Spirit be poured upon us
> from on high, and the wilderness be
> a fruitful field, and the fruitful field
> be counted for a forest.
>
> Isa. 32:15

PALMA CHRISTI (Ricinus communis)

Also known as the castor oil plant, the name palma christi was given because of the hand-like shape of the leaves.

Widespread throughout the Middle East, in such places as Iraq, the palma christi grows to a height of 15 feet.

This plant is believed to be the 'gourd' mentioned in the Book of Jonah 4:16. Infuriated that God did not destroy the wicked city of Ninevah, Jonah wanted to die. Feeling compassion for the prophet in his wretchedness, God caused this shade-giving plant to sprout up with amazing speed over the head of Jonah who was seated outside the city in a booth. The relief from the blazing sun gave Jonah bodily comfort and so calmed his spirit that he was able to regain his trust in God.

> Yet the Lord will command his lovingkindness
> in the daytime and in the night his song shall
> be with me, and my prayer unto God of my life.
>
> Psalm 42:8

PAPYRUS (Cyprus papyrus)

Papyrus is a tall, aquatic reed which grows in Southern Europe and North Africa.

Long before the birth of Christ, the Egyptians had learned to harvest the 10-15 foot high stalks from the river Nile and make them into pressed sheets for the purpose of writing.

If it had not been for the manufacture of this durable material, many of the earliest documents such as the Dead Sea scrolls would not have survived.

From the Greek language we get the word 'biblia' for payprus rolls which were exported by way of the ancient Phoenician port of Byblos on the Mediterranean coast. As time passed, the word 'biblia' began to be used as a general term for all manuscripts and books; thus, 'The Book' became known as the bible.

> Thy word is a lamp unto my feet, and a
> light unto my path.
>
> Psalm 119:105

PASSION FLOWER (G. Passiflora)

The passion flower is a tropical vine which is native to Mexico. It was used as an illustration of the instruments of the passion by Spanish missionaries to the New World.

The elements of the crucifixion found on the flower are:

The fringed corona which stands for the crown of thorns.

The column of the ovary which suggests the pillar of the cross.

The three styles are reminders of the three nails.

The five anthers represent the five wounds inflicted on Jesus' body while He was on the cross.

The ten sepals and petals symbolize the ten apostles who were present at the crucifixion, Judas and Peter being absent.

The lobed leaves present an image of the hands of the persecutors.

The long clinging tendrils relate to the scourges used to beat Jesus.

The length of time the flower blooms…three days, corresponds to the time between the crucifixion and the resurrection.

PINE (G. Pinaceae)

The pine tree is found in the Northern Hemisphere; many species grow to a height of 200 feet. The leaves are needle-shaped, the branches bear pendulous cones.

An incident involving a pine tree is linked to St. Martin of Tours. Before he became a priest, Martin was an army officer, a courageous man of action. Of the many miracles attributed to him, his run-in with a mob of heathen idol worshippers best demonstrates this side of his character. After tearing down their temple, Martin attacked a nearby pine tree which was sacred to idolaters. As his axe bit into the tree's trunk, Martin was threatened with bodily harm. Recognizing that Martin was a zealous Christian, one of the heathen threw out a challenge: "Stay the axe! We will feel the pine ourselves, but you must stand directly in the path of its fall. This will be a test for us to find out whether that God of yours is really as powerful as men claim he is, and saves his own."

Martin accepted the challenge and was tied up in the path of the pine's fall. The heathen worked feverishly to chop the tree down; when it began to topple, Martin made the sign of the cross. Miraculously the tree changed direction before crashing to the ground. Conversion of the astonished heathen followed.

POINSETTIA (Euphorbia pulcherrima)

Native to Mexico, this tropical shrub was brought to the United States in the 1800s and gradually was adopted as a floral symbol of the Christmas season.

There is a Mexican folk legend about a boy, so poor that he had absolutely nothing to bring to his parish church on Christmas Eve. Kneeling down, he apologized to God for his lack of a gift. As he scrambled to his feet, he noticed a poinsettia springing up from the ground. Snapping off some of the brilliant red bracts, he placed them on the altar with joy in his heart.

> He will listen to the prayers of the destitute. He will not reject their pleas.

> Psalm 102:17

POMEGRANATE *(Punica granatum)*

Cultivated in Palestine since biblical times, the pomegranate is a small bush-like tree. The fruit is the size of an orange.

When the Children of Israel were wandering in the wilderness, they yearned for the past comforts of Egypt, especially the juicy red pulp of the pomegranate, to slake their thirst. (Numbers 29:5) It is not surprising that the pomegranate became a symbol of life, fertility and prosperity. Representations adorned the pillars of Solomon's temple, and were embroidered onto the hem of Aaron's priestly robe.

Late, in Judeo-Christian symbolism, the many seeds enclosed within the fruit's rind represented individuals united in temple or church. The blood of martyrs is represented by the red juice.

> Behold how good and how pleasant it is
> for brethren to dwell together in unity!
>
> Psalm 133:1

PRAYER PLANT (Maranta leuconeura kerchoveana)

An ornamental foliage plant from tropical America. As darkness falls, the leaves curl upward in pairs to a vertical position, like a pair of praying hands.

Prayer brings us into God's presence; it is a personal relationship with a loving Father who knows our needs, shortcomings and desires.

Jesus prayed often, and St. Paul exhorted us to "Rejoice always, and pray without ceasing." (1 Thessalonians 5:16, 17)

Used for confession, submission, and commission, prayer can transform lives.

> And when they had prayed, the place was shaken where they were assembled together; and they were all filled with the Holy Ghost, and they spake the word of God with boldness.
>
> Acts 4:31

QUAKING ASPEN (Populus tremula)

This hardy, fast-growing tree, spread throughout Western Europe and North America, is also known as the trembling popular.

The leaves make a rustling sound when their blades, set at right angles to their long stems, become activated by the wind. According to legend, the leaves of this tree quiver because Jesus cursed it knowing that of all the trees, the aspen was the only one that refused to bow down in respect to the Holy Family during their flight into Egypt. Another theory blames the fearful quaking on the fact that the son of God Almighty was nailed to an aspen cross.

> The fear of the Lord is the beginning of wisdom.
>
> Psalm 111:10

REDBUD (G. Cercis)

In the spring, the sweet-pea shaped, purple-pink or white flowers bloom along the branches of this tree long before the appearance of the leaves.

The redbud has long been associated with biblical legend, and is often called the Judas tree.

One of the twelve disciples of Jesus, Judas Iscariot, was treasurer of the group. After Jesus and the twelve went up to Jerusalem, "Satan entered into Judas" (Luke 22:3) and he betrayed his leader for thirty pieces of silver.

Following Jesus' arrest, it is claimed that a remorseful Judas hanged himself on this kind of tree, and the flowers, which were white at that time, turned purple-pink as they burned with shame.

> O God, thou knowest my foolishness;
> and my sins are not hid from thee.
>
> Psalm 69:5

RED EVERLASTING (*Helichrysum sanguineum*)

According to Israel legend, each plant marks a spot where a Maccabean soldier shed his blood in the battle fighting against the Syrian dictator Antiochus to restore religious freedom and traditional Jewish worship.

The plant is used as a symbol for the Israeli Memorial Day honoring fallen soldiers and victims of terrorism in April or May.

A protected species, the bright red color of the red everlasting flowers does not fade when life has been taken out of them through drying.

Promise of eternal life is very rarely mentioned in the Old Testament, However, Jesus preached that life on earth is only the beginning of a life that goes on forever.

John 11:25, 26

RED POPPY (Papaver rhoeas)

Growing in the temperate regions of the world, this annual plant has a flower with four petals and a black spot at their base. It is also known as corn poppy because of its habit of re-seeding itself in grain fiends.

It should be noted that red or corn poppy is not the same as the opium poppy.

Used as a symbol of remembrance, the inspiration for which came from a poem written by a Canadian medical officer, Colonel John Mcrae while he waited for casualties from the second Battle of Ypres, it included the lines:

> In Flanders fields the poppies blow,
> between the crosses, row on row...

Published in "Punch" in 1915, the poem became widely known and was published in 1918 by "Ladies Home Journal". An American woman, Moina Michaels, was greatly touched by this and on the day the armistice was signed, bought a bunch of red paper poppies from a New York department store and handed them to delegates attending a Y.M.C.A. leader's conference, to remind them of the fallen. As is well known, the idea took off, and is still followed to this day, proceeds going to help veterans and their families.

RESURRECTION PLANT (Selaginella lepidophyllia)

The dictionary describes the word 'resurrection' as rising from the dead or returning to life. This relates perfectly to the action of this fern-like desert plant.

Native to the arid regions of southern Texas and Mexico, it has fronds which roll up into a ball, brownish and dead-looking, during excessive dry spells, and which unfold and turn green throughout periods of rain.

According to legend, it is said that this plant displayed its minute white flowers and became green when the Christ child was born, closed into a brown ball at His crucifixion, and opened again in all its glory to celebrate Easter; hence its name.

> Jesus said unto her, (Martha), I am the resurrection, and the life: he that believeth in me, though he were dead, yet shall he live:
>
> John 11:25

ROGATION FLOWER (*Polygala vulgaris*)

This plant is also called milkwort because of its supposed ability to increase human lactation.

According to the English Church calendar, rogation days are the Monday, Tuesday, and Wednesday preceding Ascension Day. The word 'rogation' comes from the Latin 'rogare' to ask.

Processions bearing garlands and nosegays of blue, white and pink rogation flowers process along the edges of the sprouting fields while chanting prayers of supplication for a successful harvest.

> Be patient therefore, brethren, unto the coming of the Lord. Behold, the husbandman waiteth for the precious fruit of the earth, and hath long patience for it, until he receive the early and latter rain.
>
> James 5:7

ROSE (G. Rosa)

The rose with its beauty and fragrance has been a favorite since ancient times.

In the 12th Century, the abbot and theologian Bernard of Clairvaux declared that the white rose should stand for the Virgin Mary's virginity and love of God, the red rose for her charity and compassion.

In the chivalric medieval secular world, a white rose represented death, and a red rose passionate love.

According to Italian legend, God showed his love to Saint Rita of Cascia using a rose. As this pious nun lay dying in the winter of 1447, she asked a friend to fetch a rose from a garden she had once cared for. The friend was perplexed as roses were out of season, but she went anyway. Miraculously, she found a single bloom.

> And the desert shall rejoice and blossom as the rose.
>
> Is. 35:1

ROSEMARY (*Rosmarinus officinalis*)

The Latin name for this evergreen shrub with aromatic leaves is derived from ros = dew and marinus = sea.

Besides being cultivated in many parts of the temperate zone for culinary purposes and perfume manufacture, this shrub can be found growing wild on the sea cliffs of Southern Europe. According to legend, the white flowers were said to have changed to pale blue when Mary hung her newly washed robe to dry on a rosemary bush during the Holy Family's flight into Egypt. Ancient people believed that rosemary improved memory, and it came to symbolize remembrance of the dead...hence the custom of placing a sprig on a loved one's grave.

"ROSE OF SHARON" ... *Autumn crocus (Colchhicum autumnale)*

"I am the rose of Sharon, and the lily of the valleys."

Song of Sol. 2:1

Scholars disagree about the identity of this flower. Is it the deep red Tulipa Montana that grows in the hills of Sharon? Is it the Sea Daffodil (Pancratium maritimum) whose white flowers shoot up out of the sand above the tide-line on the coast which borders the Sharon Plain?

The RSV calls it "autumn crocus". I'm going with this, the most recent interpretation, as I photographed it's beauty long before I started this book, and kept it, only God knew why.

ST. ANDREW'S CROSS (Ascyrum hypericoides)

St. Andrew's cross is a plant which grows on the rocky, sandy soil of the eastern coastal plain of the United States. It is so named because its yellow oblong petals form an oblique cross.

Andrew earned his living as a fisherman. He lived at Bethsaida on the Sea of Galilee. It was there that he became the first disciple of Jesus. From then on, he became a follower, one of the twelve apostles. After the death of Jesus, Andrew became a missionary. He was arrested and executed cruelly on an x-shaped cross at Patras in Greece on the orders of a Roman pro-consul whose wife refused conjugal relations after Andrew had converted her to the Christian faith.

During the 4th Century, Regulus, a monk of Patras had a dream in which an angel told him that the Emperor Constantine was planning to move the bones of St. Andrew to Constantinople.

St. Regulus fled to Scotland with the holy relics and founded a settlement named St. Andrews on the coast of Fife.

During the 8th Century, a legend circulated regarding the Pictish King Oengus MacFergus who prayed to St. Andrew for help against invaders. An x-shaped cross appeared in the sky, and the King and his soldiers were victorious.

ST. BARBARA'S HERB (G. Barbarea)

Also known as yellow rocket or winter-cress, this plant belongs to the mustard family. The stem bears glossy lobed leaves which are edible in the winter months. In certain countries, the leaves are picked for use in salads.

According to a 7th Century legend, the saint this flower honors was a beautiful maiden whose father kept her prisoner in a tower to deter her many suitors. On hearing that she had become a Christian, her pagan father tried to have her killed, but by some miracle she was spirited out of reach at every attempt. Frustrated, he turned her over to the authorities for torture, but she held onto her Christian faith. Finally, her father was ordered to kill her himself which he did with a beheading.

After this grisly deed, a great storm swept down on the scene. Barbara's father was struck by a lightning bolt and all that remained of him was a heap of ashes. For this reason, St. Barbara became the patron saint of artillery regiments.

> For it is indeed just of God to repay with affliction those who afflict you.
>
> 2 Thess. 1:6
> NRSV, 1989

ST. BRUNO'S LILY (Anthericum liliastrum)

Growing from a bulb, this sweet-scented plant has pristine white trumpet flowers with yellow or dark orange anthers. It is native to the European Alps where Bruno spent part of his life. This saint, of French stock, was born in Cologne, Germany c. 1030 A.D. After studying at the Cathedral School in Rheims, France, he was ordained a priest, and taught theology there for 20 years.

Things changed, his career hit a road block and he was relieved of his post as master of archdiocesan schools because he had denounced his archbishop for obtaining the see of Rheims through the buying and selling of ecclesiastical offices and pardons.

Deeply saddened, Bruno and six companions left Rheims and headed for the wild seclusion of the French Alps. Soon after, he built a church, and founded a religious community which later spread to become a worldwide order of Carthusian monks.

St. Bruno's road block and successful recovery from it is an example of a divine purpose at work that will not let disaster have the last word.

ST. DABEOC'S HEATH (*Daboecia cantabrica*)

A low-growing heather-like plant, native to Ireland; the leaves of this heath are evergreen with silvery undersides. It produces white, pink or purple flowers.

St. Dabeoc has been dubbed an obscure saint...his name does not even make the long official list of saints among the Irish. However, obscure or not, St. Dabeoc has been perpetuated through the naming of the plant after him.

The saint lived during the early days of the church in a beautiful part of Ireland, Donegal in the north-west. Here, his name is associated with a place called Kilteevogue, the modern pronunciation of Kill-Dabeoc, meaning the church of Dabeoc. His name is also linked to nearby Loch Derg.

His struggle to convert the pagans must have been successful for Dabeoc to be remembered in this way. Perhaps he used twigs of this hardy plant to sprinkle holy water on his converts, much in the manner of Eastern Orthodox priests who use juniper twigs to bless people with holy water.

ST. GEORGE'S MUSHROOM (Calocybe gambosa)

This edible, creamy-white mushroom grows in circles or groups beside hedges or in open fields with non-acidic soil. It is ripe for picking in late April, hence its name is linked to St George, the soldier-saint, whose feast day is celebrated in England on April 23rd. Who was St. George? He certainly had nothing to do with mushrooms. He is regarded as a mystery man who was believed to have slain a dragon to save a princess from harm This took place in Libya between the 3rd and 4th centuries, and was said to have led to the Christianization of most of that kingdom.

Later, George was beheaded because of his Christian faith, at Lydda in Palestine.

> Watch ye, stand fast in the faith,
> quit you like men, be strong.
>
> 1 Cor. 16:13

ST. JOHN'S WORT (Hypericum)

This plant with its yellow, sun-like flowers got its name because it blooms around June 24th, St. John the Baptist's Day. During this festival its sprigs were picked to be worn, or hung on the front door to ward off the devil. On the day the saint was beheaded, red spots are said to appear on the root, symbolizing his blood.

Grown throughout the Northern Hemisphere, recent clinical and laboratory research has earned St. John's wort a reputation as a remedy for moderate depression.

The Bible teaches that, in the long run, we need more than dependency on such things as pills and music therapy; in order to find true inner peace, we need to find Jesus Christ.

SAXIFRAGE (G. Saxifraga)

Those saxifrages which grow in the wild have mats of toothed, rounded leaves situated below hairy, erect flower stalks. The small, white to greenish flowers start blooming in April.

This plant fits its name so perfectly, growing out of a cleft in the rock. In Latin, saxifraga means rock-breaker, it follows, therefore, that the plant was so named because it was thought by the ancients that it had the ability to split rocks while rooting.

In the Bible, God is referred to as a rock because of his great strength and availability as a place of refuge from one's enemies.

> For who is God, save the Lord?
> And who is a rock, save our God?
>
> Samuel 22:32

God is always there for us, solid as a rock. Hold fast!

SCABIOUS (G. Scabiosa)

Also known as devil's bit or pincushion flower, this plant is native to Europe but has been naturalized in North America. The rounded flower heads are usually blue, lavender or pink.

The root, once famed for its curative power, has a stunted appearance. European superstition linked the wild scabious to the devil who was said to have bitten off the end of the root in the hope that it would cure the sweats which afflicted him whenever he thought about his fate on the Day of Judgment.

> And the devil who had deceived them
> was thrown into the lake of fire and
> sulfur, where the beast and the false
> prophet were, and they will be tormented
> day and night forever and ever.

Rev. 20:10
NRSV, 1989

SEASONING HERBS...Mint (G Mentha); Anise (Pimpinella anisum); Cumin (Cuminum cyminum)

At the time of Christ, the spice trade was monopolized by the people of the Mid-East. Mint leaves were used to flavor food and drink, anise (or dill) seed was mixed into dough for bread, and cumin seed was used to spice up meat.

Jesus mentioned spices when he vented his anger on the scribes and Pharisees who religiously gave God a tenth of their seasoning herbs.

> Woe unto you scribes and Pharisees, hypocrites! For ye pay tithes of mint, and anise and cumin, and have omitted the weightier matters of the law, judgment, money, and faith: these ought ye to have done, and not leave the other undone.
>
> Matt. 23:23

SELF-HEAL *(Prunella vulgaris)*

This hardy perennial of European origin grows in woods, pastures and waste places. It was so named because of its reputed healing powers, though there is not much evidence that it is effective. Today, there are wonder drugs which can cure some things; and there is another road to healing called faith.

Many of the miracles of Jesus involved people who were sick with incurable diseases because folk medicine did not work.

The healing of the woman with the hemorrhage involved personal faith. (Matt. 9:21, 22). The recovery of the centurion's paralyzed servant bears testament to a different road to healing, namely the faith of another person. (Matt. 8:13).

SNOWDROP (Galanthus nivalis)

These delicate, bell-shaped, white flowers grow to a height of 4-7 inches. They appear from midwinter to early spring. There is a legend linked to snowdrops. After Eve was expelled from the Garden of Eden, she was deeply troubled; to add to her despairing mood, the landscape was brown and barren. Suddenly, snow began to fall and soon it beautified the earth with a white blanket. An angel appeared; as he comforted Eve, he stretched out his arm to catch a falling snowflake which turned into a white flower. He then bounded upward and flew away back to heaven leaving behind a cluster of snowdrops on the spot where his feet had touched the ground.

> For the Lord will not
> > reject forever.
>
> Although he causes grief, he will have
> > compassion
> according to the abundance of his
> steadfast love:
>
> for he does not willingly afflict
> > or grieve anyone.

Lam. 3:31-33
NRSV, 1989

SOLOMON'S SEAL (G. Polugonatum)

Solomon's seal is a herb of the lily family. Its name is suggested either by the seal-like scars left where old stems have broken off the rootstock, or its medicinal use of healing wounds.

Israel's King Solomon was granted divine wisdom in answer to a humble prayer. His judgments and his seal of approval became widely respected.

> For wisdom is better than rubies;
> and all the things that may be desired
> are not to be compared to it.

Proverbs 8:11

Some judgments have to be made by us as individuals. An attitude of indifference, of letting everything be decided for us by officialdom, is not the Christian way. That is why we must ask God for wisdom in our prayers.

SPIKENARD (*Nardostachys jatamansi*)

An aromatic plant native to India, also called 'nard'. It has rose-purple flowers.

A fragrant oil was extracted from the plant and exported to the Holy Land in sealed alabaster jars to preserve the perfume. The jars were high-priced, each one costing the equivalent of a laborer's yearly compensation.

> Now when Jesus was in Bethany, in the house of Simon the leper, there came unto him a woman having an alabaster box of very precious ointment, and poured it on his head, as he sat at meat.
> But when his disciples saw it, they had indignation, saying: To what purpose is this waste?
> For this ointment might have been sold for much, and given to the poor.
> When Jesus understood it, he said unto them: Why trouble ye the woman? For for she hath wrought a good work upon me.
> For ye have the poor always with you; But me ye have not always. For in that she hath poured this ointment on my body, she did it for my burial.
> Verily I say unto you: Wheresoever this Gospel shall be preached in the whole world, there shall also this, that this woman hath done, be told for a memorial of her.
>
> (Matt. 26:6-13)

Besides recognizing the woman's love, Jesus showed love for his disciples at this time, by preparing them for his imminent death.

STAR THISTLE (Centaurea calcitrapa)

This plant has yellow or red-purple flowers and bracts ending in a star pattern of long spurs and smaller spines.

The legend connected to this plant is set in Bethlehem. A man, while weeding his plot of land, dug up a star thistle and tried to get rid of it by tossing it onto a nearby path. It landed in front of none other than the Virgin Mary who happened to be passing by. She told him to replant it, and that through the ages to come it would be cherished. Was this a foretelling of the piercing of her son's flesh by spears and nails, followed by His resurrection to become the savior of mankind?

> In this way God fulfilled what he had foretold through all the prophets, that his Messiah would suffer.

>> Acts 3:18
>> NRSV, 1989

STORAX *(Styrax officinalis)*

A tree native to the Mediterranean area, the resin from the bark is used in the manufacture of perfume.

Arabs deem this tree to be sacred and have connected it to a legend. Moses, escaping from Pharaoh and his army through the desert was forced to halt because of exhaustion. He drove his staff made of storax wood into the ground, and as he rested, the staff miraculously sprouted leaf-bearing branches which shaded him from the merciless rays of the sun.

> Behold, the eye of the Lord is upon them
> that fear him, upon them that hope
> in his mercy;
> To deliver their soul from death, and keep
> them alive in famine.

Psalm 33:18, 19

SYCAMORE (Acer pseudoplatanus)

In Old Testament times a tree of this name was so common that King Solomon "made cedars as abundant as the sycamores that are in the lowland." (1 Kings 10:27)

Although not related to the Palestinian sycamores, a tree bearing the same name is common in North America and Europe. The Northern Hemisphere tree in linked to an Irish legend that demonstrated man's reliance on God's gift of pure water.

At Cloneeagh near Maryborough in Leix, a sycamore grew near a well at the site of a monastery whose abbot was the revered St. Fintan (d. 603).

In time, when the well got polluted by animals who were allowed to drink there, it miraculously transferred to another of St. Fintan's religious houses at Cromogne, just three miles distant. Water was always in the cavity of this sycamore, even during a drought. It was believed to filter up from an underground spring through pores in the trunk. The water was regarded as holy, not only for its constancy, but also it gave relief to people afflicted with weak eyesight and other ailments.

> Then the lame man shall leap as an hart,
> and the tongue of the dumb sing: for in
> the wilderness shall waters break out,
> and streams in the desert.
> And the parched ground shall become a pool,
> and the thirsty land springs of water...Isaiah 35:6, 7

TEREBINTH (Pistachia terebinthus)

Common in the Holy Land, this tree has broad, spreading branches, and grows 35 feet in height. It also has an astonishing long life, some reaching 1,000 years. Its Hebrew name is "elah" which embodies the Canaanite word of 'el', meaning God, along with the oak whose Hebrew name is 'alon'. Both trees were regarded as sacred. They were the prized location for altars, burials, and the hiding of treasure.

Two miles north of Hebron, archaeologists have unearthed the the remains of a scorched altar and the roots of a terebinth tree. This site, linked to Abraham, is a stopping place for pilgrims. The heathen also loved the deep shade of these mighty trees. The prophet Ezekiel denounced their ungodly practices there.

> Then shall ye know that I am the Lord,
> when their slain men shall be among
> their idols round about their altars,
> upon every high hill, in all the tops of
> the mountains, and under every green
> tree, and under every thick oak, the place
> where they did offer sweet savor to all
> their idols.
>
> Ezek. 6:13

THORNS & THISTLES (Various)

Jesus said: "Ye shall know them by their fruits. Do men gather grapes of thorns, or figs of thistles?"

Corrupt fruit cannot grow from a healthy tree, neither can an unhealthy tree produce good fruit. Every rotten tree should be cut down and burned.

If we are subject to the will of the Father, then we will be given the power to distinguish good from heavily disguised evil. If we are in his camp, we will understand.

VERONICA (G. Veronica)

Veronica, also named speedwell, is a genus of plants and shrubs. They are believed to be named after the legendary woman of Jerusalem who performed a good deed. Filled with compassion at the sight of the suffering Jesus on his way to his execution, she wiped His perspiring face with a handkerchief, since called a veronica, meaning "true likeness". Afterwards, she was amazed to discover that His features were impressed on the cloth; the form and markings on the flowers of some of this genus were thought to match. Although her true identity was never discovered, Veronica, as she came to be known, was made a saint.

> God blesses those who are merciful,
> for they will be shown mercy.
>
> Matt. 5:7

VERVAIN (G. Verbena)

Variations of this herbaceous plant are known the world over. It's phlox-like flowers can be purple, blue, red, white or yellow. Renowned for its medicinal properties, legend has it that vervain, also known as Herb-of-the-Cross, was used at the crucifixion to staunch Christ's wounds.

In the Middle Ages, the plant was worn as a pledge of good faith, a badge sported by heralds and ambassadors as they went about their business.

St. Paul exhorted Christians to be:

>ambassadors for Christ...openly speaking
>for Him as messengers.

2 Corinthians 5:20

VIOLET (G. Viola)

Thee are over 500 species of this low growing plant worldwide. The flowers have five dainty petals which are blue-purple, white or yellow. The violet blooms from March through June, mostly in woodland and moist fields.

According to legend, the once upright violet was so overwhelmed by the shameful nature of Christ's crucifixion that it bowed its head when the shadow of the cross fell on Golgotha where it grew. Sadly, the plant never recovered, and bows its head to this day.

King David, presumably in his later years, gives wise advice when he tells us not to fret because of the doings of evil men. (Psalm 37:1)

WALNUT (G. Juglans)

The walnut tree is valued for its dark brown wood and edible nuts. St. Augustine of Hippo describes its fruit having three distinct parts. The outer shell stands for the wood of the cross; the nut stands for the flesh of Christ with the bitterness of suffering; the kernel represents the divine revelation which nourishes us...its oil is used to give light.

Dictionaries define 'revelation' as an enlightening, astonishing disclosure. The divine revelation is the voice of God speaking to us... He speaks directly to us so that we can spread the light.

> "...both with signs and wonders, with various miracles, and gifts of the Holy Spirit."
>
> Hebrews 2:4

WANDERING JEW (Zebrina pendula)

A trailing house plant with variegated leaves, native to tropical America. It is named after a legendary person.

When Christ was passing along the street bearing his cross to Calvary, a voice from the crowd of onlookers cried "Go faster! A little speed!" Jesus turned round and answered this scornful remark: "I truly am going, but you will be waiting when I return." Ever since that day, according to a medieval legend, the Jew who made that gibe wanders the earth consumed with remorse. At the end of every century, he is said to become gravely ill and falls into a trance. When he comes to, he is the same youthful age that he was when he scoffed at Jesus.

> For he is the minister of God to thee for good.
> But if thou do that which is evil, be afraid;
> for he beareth not the sword in vain; for he is
> the minister of God, a revenger to execute wrath
> upon him that doeth evil.
>
>   Romans 13:5

WEEPING WILLOW (Salix babylonica)

> By the rivers of Babylon, there we
> sat down, yea, we wept, when we
> remembered Zion.
>
> We hanged our harps upon the
> willows in the midst thereof.
>
> Psalm 173:1, 2

Although scholars now believe that the willow mentioned in the above psalm, is, in fact, the Euphrates aspen, this tree of the riverbank with its drooping branches, still holds sway in the popular imagination as a symbol of grief.

One of this tree's other attributes is its resilience...cut off its shoots and it will continue to thrive. Thus it has also come to stand for the gospel, which, unceasingly, is spread throughout the world, despite ongoing persecutions.

> And they departed, and went through the towns,
> preaching the gospel, and healing everywhere.
>
> Luke 9:6

WHEAT (G. Triticum)

Cultivated since the beginning of civilization, wheat has always been a premier grain for bread making.

In the eyes of the Israelites it was a symbol of God's bounty. The crop flourished in the Philistine plain, the Jordan valley and the Plain of Jezreel. In late spring or early summer, the stalks were cut with sickles and bundled into sheaves to be taken to the threshing floor.

In Christian symbolism, wheat represents Christ who is "the bread of life."

It is interesting to note that the name Bethlehem, Christ's birthplace, means in Hebrew, "the house of bread."

WHITE LILY (Lilium candidum)

The white, or madonna lily has been dedicated by the Church to the Virgin Mary. It is regarded as a symbol of purity and chastity. There is a legend linking the lily to the betrothal of Mary and Joseph. Zacharius, the high priest, enquired of God about Mary; presumably because his son was interested in the maiden. In reply, an angel told Zacharius to send out a call to all interested widowers; they were to come to the temple carrying their staffs. There God would give a sign as to who was to be Mary's husband. The next morning, Joseph's staff was found to have blossomed with white lilies. The losing suitors broke their staffs in two and stormed out.

> Call unto me, and I will answer thee,
> and shew thee great and mighty things,
> which thou knowest not.
>
> Jeremiah 33:3

WOOD SORREL (G. Oxalis)

A spreading plant found in the fields as well as woods, wood sorrel, with its compound leaf composed of three leaflets, is one of the three closely linked plants, the others being clover and shamrock. When St. Patrick was a slave-shepherd during his youth, he had the opportunity to familiarize himself with the plants of the Irish countryside. Later on, when he became a missionary to the pagan Irish rural dwellers, he used them as a teaching symbol to explain the Holy Trinity.

Another candidate for this honor is watercress (Rorippa nasturtium-aquaticum) sometimes named St. Patrick's cabbage, which is capable of producing three leaflets that could have been utilized by the Saint. The norm for this watercress is four leaflets, so one can imagine that before one of St. Patrick's sermons, a follower, ankle-deep in a stream or well, fishing for the three-leafed ones...or as this is an edible plant, they could have been found at a market stall or on the dinner table.

Patrick's concept of the Holy Trinity was handed down by the first ecclesiastical council which met at Nicaea, a city in the eastern Roman empire, in 325 A.D.

WORMWOOD (Artemesia absinthium)

Wormwood is an aromatic herb or shrub, also known in the British Isles and Europe as mugwort or St. John's herb, the latter because it was associated with the ceremonies of St. John's Eve, and was said to ward off evil spirits.

In the Bible, wormwood appears as a metaphor for a bitter calamity:

> He hath filled me with bitterness,
> he hath made me drunken with wormwood.
>
> Remembering my affliction and my misery,
> the wormwood and the gall.
>
> Lamentations 3:15 & 19

In 1986, a nuclear meltdown in the form of fires and explosions occurred at a power plant called Chernobyl in Ukraine, scatting radioactive particles all over Europe. Translated into English, Chernobyl means wormwood. The place was given this name because the herb grew on the banks of the nearby Dneiper river. Thousands died from cancers and related diseases as a result of the accident. Fifteen years later, nearly 2,000 cases of thyroid cancer linked to the Chernobyl disaster were still being reported.

> And the name of the star is called
> Wormwood: and the third part of
> the waters became wormwood: and
> many died of the waters, because they
> were made bitter.
>
> (Rev. 8:11)

YELLOW ARCHANGEL *(Lamiastrum galeobdolon)*

This evergreen ground cover with silver-marked foliage is hardy enough to thrive under trees. The yellow flowers bloom from late spring into early summer.

In the biblical realm, archangels are one rank above angels. According to the apocrypha, they are:

> "the seven holy angels, which
> present the prayers of the saints,
> and which go in and out before
> the glory of the Holy One."
>
> Tob. 12:15

The seven, whose names are Uriel, Michael, Jeremial, Gabriel, Raphael, Raguel and Sariel, are also mentioned in the Book of Revelation 8:2, 6.

Archangels are sent to perform important tasks and to deliver important messages as when the Angel Gabriel was sent to Zacharius and Mary. (Luke 1:19, 26)

YELLOW GENTIAN (European) Gentiana lutea)

St. Ladislas the First became King of Hungary in 1077, following in the footsteps of St. Stephen. His army defeated the pagan Cumans and Pechenegs who were forced to settle in designated areas and accept Christ. Just and virtuous, King Ladislas instigated a new legal code.

There is a legend surrounding the King; when his country was ravaged by a plague, he shot an arrow into the air and implored God to guide it to a plant whose medicinal properties would save his people; it fell on the yellow gentian, a meadow herb, renowned for the healing power of its roots.

Our Lord God says:

> He shall call upon me,
> and I will answer him: I will
> be with him in trouble; I will
> deliver him, and honor him."

Psalm 91:15

YEW (G. Taxus)

This tree or evergreen shrub has flat needles and red, berrylike fruits. The reason that yew trees are often found in churchyards is two fold. Firstly, the early Christians planted the yew around their churches as symbols of everlasting life. Secondly, the wood was highly treasured, being used for the making of the successful war weapon the English longbow.

Before the time of enclosures, the churchyard was the only place in the village that was fenced off from grazing animals who would have been poisoned if they had chewed on yew. The fact that archers practiced within the confines of the churchyard is borne out by long, deep scratches on the sandstone walls of some early churches where they had paused to sharpen their arrows.

> He teacheth my hands to war; so that a bow of steel
> is broken by mine arms
>
> Thou hast also given me the shield of thy salvation:
> and thy gentleness hath made me great.
>
> 2 Samuel 22:35, 36

About the author.

Hilary Giner-Sorolla spent her childhood in Cleveland, U.K. which is a county sandwiched between Durham and North Yorkshire. She presently makes her home in Western North Carolina.

Hilary's writing credits include six screenplays, a novella and magazine articles. This is her first non-fiction book. Reading about flowers and trees and their stories, she was struck by the predominance of Roman and Greek legends so she decided to give Christian legends a fair shake. She found plenty of material...enough to make it worthwhile. "This is a book for all ages, lovers of beauty and nature enquirers, legend aficionados and seekers of truth. Above all, it is a celebration of the glory of God."

BIBLIOGRAPHY

Moldenke, Harold & Alma – Plants of the Bible (Dover, 1952)

Wells, Diana – 100 Flowers & How They Got Their Names – Algonquin, 1997

Friend, Hilderic – Flower Lore, 1884. Copyright Para Research, Inc.

Attwater, Donald with John, Catherine Rachel. The Penguin Dictionary of Saints, 1995

Walker, Winifred – All the Plants of the Bible – Harper & Bros. c 1957

Everyday Life in New Testament Times – Batsford Ltd. 1954

John, Catherine Rachel – The Saints of Cornwall, 1981

Treharne, R.F. – The Glastonbury Legends, Cresset Press, 1967

Watkin, E.I. – Neglected Saints – Sheed & Ward, 1955

Hanaurer, J.E. – Folklore of the Holy Land, Moslem, Christian & Jewish – Dover, 2002

Smith, A.W. – A Gardener's Handbook of Plant Names, Their Meaning & Origins -- Dover, 1997

Talbot, C.H. – Anglo-Saxon Missionaries in Germany – Sheed & Ward, 1954

Lockyer, Herbert – All the Parables of the Bible – Zondervan, 1963

Vickery, Roy – Oxford Dictionary of Plant Lore, Oxford University Press, 1995

Oxford English Dictionary, 2nd Edition, 1989

Who's Who in the Bible – Reader's Digest, 1994

Avigad, Brakha & Danin, Avinoam – Flowers of Jerusalem – E. Lewin-Epstein, 1972

Biederman, Hans – Dictionary of Symbolism. Facts on File, Inc. 1992

Treharne, R.F. -- The Glastonbury Legends. Cresset Press, 1967

Fleming, Daniel Johnson – Christian Symbols in a World Community. Friendship Press, 1940

Keller, W. – The Bible as History. Hodder & Stoughton, 1956

Skinner, Charles M. – Myths & Legends of Flowers, Trees, Fruits, and Plants. Fredonia Books, Amsterdam, The Netherlands.

Thurston, Herbert J. & Attwater, Donald – Butler's Lives of the Saints. P.J. Kenedy & Sons, N.Y., 1956

The American Heritage Dictionary of the English Language. Houghton Mifflin, Co. 1975

Clement, Clara Erskine. Christian Symbols & Stories of the Saints as Illustrated in Art. Houghton Mifflin 1886

Gordon, Lesley – Green Magic. Flowers, Plants & Herbs in Lore & Legend. Ebury Press. Copyright Webb & Bower, Ltd. 1977

Lockyer, Herbert – All the Miracles of the Bible. Zondervan Publishing House, 1961

Lehner, E.&J. – Folklore & Symbolism of Flowers, Plants & Trees. Dover Pictorial Archives Series, 2003. Republication 1960, Tudor Publishing, N.Y., 1960

Martin, W. Keble – The Concise British Flora in Colour. George Rainbird. Copyright, 1965

Gandolfi, Claudine – Little Christmas Treasures. Peter Pauper Press, Inc. White Plains, N.Y. 1997

Illustrated Dictionary & Concordance of the Bible – The Jerusalem Publishing House, Ltd. 1986

Lang, J. Stephen -- The Complete Book of Bible Promises. Tyndale House Publishers, Inc. 1997

Duersen. A. Van – Illustrated Dictionary of Bible Manners & Customs. Citadel Press. 1967.

Coffin, Tristram P. -- The Book of Christian Folklore, Seabury Press, 1973.

British Heritage Magazine, July 2005.

Steffler, Alva William – Symbols of the Christian Faith. William B. Eerdmans Publishing Co. 2002.

Ammer, Christine – American Dictionary of Idioms, Houghton Mifflin Co. 1997

Random House. Webster's Unabridged Dictionary, 2nd edition. 1998.

Georgia, Ada – Manual of Weeds, the Macmillan Co. 1933.

Polese, Jean-Marie – The Pocket Guide to Mushrooms, Konemann. 2005.

Azaria, Alon – The Natural History of the Land of the Bible, The Jerusalem Publishing House, Ltd. 1969.

Tradigo, Alfredo (translated by Stephen Sartarelli) – Icons & Saints of the Eastern Orthodox Church, J. Paul Getty Museum, Los Angeles. 2006.

Hulme, F. Edward & Hibberd, Shirley – Familiar Garden Flowers, 3rd series, Cassell & Company, Ltd. (no date given).

CPSIA information can be obtained
at www.ICGtesting.com
Printed in the USA
243100LV00002B